Acclaim for this book

"You meet someone on the Internet *{or anywhere}* who seems to be your perfect partner. You have so much in common. You share the same values. This person proclaims unending love. You fall for him or her, meet in person, and agree to have sexual relations. Later you learn that your lover is not at all the person he or she pretended to be. So did you really consent to sex with this individual?

Joyce Short says, "No, you did not." In *Combatting Romance Scams – Why Lying to Get Laid Is a Crime!* she clearly argues that when people misrepresent their identities in order to seduce their targets, they are sexual predators and should be prosecuted. Although some states have laws that can be used to punish these predators, Ms. Short wants to see romance scam laws enacted in order to protect the sanctity of your body. It's a vital message that should be communicated to lawmakers everywhere."

—**Donna Andersen**, author of *Lovefraud.com*

COMBATING
Romance
SCAMS

Also by Joyce M. Short:

Carnal Abuse by Deceit
How a Predator's Lies Became Rape

COMBATING *Romance* SCAMS

Why Lying to Get Laid Is a Crime!

JOYCE SHORT

Copyright, 2016, Joyce M. Short

All rights reserved.
Except as permitted under the U.S. Copyright Act of 1976, no portion of this publication may be reproduced or transmitted in any form or by any means, or stored in a database or retrieval system, without the express written permission of the author/illustrator and publisher.

Publisher: Pandargos Press
New York, NY, USA

Email: StopRomaceScams@yahoo.com

ISBN: 978-0-692-82439-9

Author/Illustrator: Joyce M. Short
Cover and Book Design: Author Support

Dedicated to my son because opinions don't change without enlightenment. He's my inspiration.

Table of Contents

INTRODUCTION		xi
CHAPTER 1	*Romance Scams and the 800-Pound Gorilla in the Room*	1
CHAPTER 2	*How and Why People Become Scammers*	13
CHAPTER 3	*Baiting the Hook: How We Get Reeled In*	20
CHAPTER 4	*Were You Seduced, or Were You "Sexploited?" How Can You Tell?*	29
CHAPTER 5	*Debunking the Heart Myth*	43
CHAPTER 6	*Blame, Shame, and Recovery*	49
CHAPTER 7	*Swimming Free: Steps to Reclaim Your Self-Esteem and Your Life*	54
CHAPTER 8	*When Lies Become Fraud*	61
CHAPTER 9	*Enacting a Romance Scam Law*	70
CHAPTER 10	*Ready, Set...Legal Action!*	81
CHAPTER 11	*What Can You Do?*	88
CHAPTER 12	*Resources to Help You Unhook*	94
DEFINITIONS		99
NOTES		107

"Then again, the very fact that he uses not force but persuasion makes him more detestable, because a lover who uses force proves himself a villain, but the one who uses persuasion ruins the character of {the victim} the one who consents."

—S<small>OCRATES</small>

"Law protects the gullible as well as the sophisticated."

—E<small>RIC</small> S<small>CHNEIDERMAN</small>
New York State Attorney General, June 2, 2016

Introduction

I was caught in a romance scam, and didn't know how badly I'd been "hooked" 'til three and a half years later. Romance scams take place all over the world, every day. It happens to women, and it happens to men.

Often society thinks that when you've been scammed for sex, it's just "entertainment." When a victim recently tried to report this crime to the police, the officer said, "You had fun, didn't you?" He totally ignored that her reproductive organs had been shamelessly violated by a sexual predator.

When it happened to me, I didn't understand either. There was no internet. There were no books that spoke of the evil behind the use of fraud in sexual exploitation. I wrote my first book, *Carnal Abuse by Deceit*, in order to give society the words to discuss this defiling crime and demonstrate the impacts on the victim. I've written *Combating Romance Scams* to provide the concepts, language and law to make romance scams stop.

I struggled for years trying to make sense of what had happened to me and deal with its fallout. People often think that when you learn you've been lied to, you can simply walk away. They know little about how the brain chemistry of attraction, trust and romance actually works. And they don't contemplate how having a child with a sexual predator, a very real possibility, can alter your entire life.

Whether a child results or not, sexual exploitation is abuse that will unhinge your very soul. Shouldn't any covert and deliberate behavior, that can so totally undermine your psyche, be a punishable offense? I've written this book to provide the facts and enable you to be the judge.

Romance Scams and the 800 Pound Gorilla in the Room

Romance scams run rampant on the internet. The Web is not the only device scammers employ. They can find you while you're walking your dog in the park, standing by the water cooler in your office, working-out at your gym, or a myriad of other ways. But if you're using Facebook, any e-dating service, or electronic communications to find a relationship, you have better than a 50% chance of being lied to and getting caught in a scam. The CEO of *Beautiful People,* an elite dating site, reported that 53% of the profiles on his very own service contained lies.[1]

Catfish is the name that's been ascribed to romance scammers who use electronic sources to troll for hook-ups. The term has its roots in the concept of *phishing*, a technique used by con artists to trick people into giving away their credit card details, Social Security numbers, or other personal data. Scammers who target people by pretending to be a specific person rather than a business, non-profit, or large corporate entity are known as *spear phishers*. Their direct approach is so powerful that they account for approximately 91% of successful scams on the internet today.[2]

Human resource managers use the concept of "The Catfish Effect" to upgrade a weak employee's performance through competition. The idea sprang from the tale of a Norwegian fisherman who added a catfish to his sardine tanks to chase his catch and keep them active until they reached port. Doing so made the fish tastier and better textured, improving his profits.

The "Catfish" concept went mainstream in 2010, when Max Joseph and Yaniv "Nev" Schulman created a movie by that name. They also produced the follow-up television docudrama that currently airs on MTV. In their series, victims fall prey without meeting the catfish who conned them until they're suspicious or aware they've been scammed. They contact Shulman and Joseph to locate the predator at the other end of the line that hooked them. But in real life, catfish profiles can result in the victim meeting the offender and carrying out an actual person-to-person sexual relationship over an extended period without their knowing they've been scammed.

To Schulman and Joseph, their concept of an emotional predator chasing a target on the internet was an easy stretch. So the term "catphishing" became "catfishing" when describing romance scams. Society owes a debt of gratitude to Schulman and Joseph for focusing interest on this topic. Whether we express the term as *catfish* or *catphish,* predators who use fake internet identities or post false descriptions (*false personation*), to embroil victims in romance scams, create considerable injury.

A catfish you don't meet harms you by misusing your trust and emotions. A scammer who engages you in a personal, sexual relationship not only misuses your trust, but also commits sexual assault by deceptively undermining your self-determination over your reproductive organs. The use of false pretense to engage you in sex invalidates your consent. Deceptions should be corrected *before* physical intimacy takes place.

The Urban Dictionary defines *catfish* as "someone who pretends to be someone they're not, using Facebook or other social media, to create false identities, particularly to pursue deceptive online romances."[3]

Society's collective monetary damages from romance scams run into billions of dollars. In November 2015 alone, $1,027,759 in losses were reported to the Australian Competition and Consumer Commission (ACCC), an agency overseen by the Australasian Consumer Frauds Task Force.[4]

The numbers for the US are staggering! The FBI reported $82 million in romance scam damages in a six month period. Approximately 82% of the victims were women and 18% were men. These numbers were taken from reported complaints. There is no way to calculate society's total, combined, actual monetary losses.[5]

The cost of treatment is not reflected in the FBI's figures.

Recovering victims often spend thousands of dollars on therapy. Many suffer from depression and may also experience symptoms similar to Post Traumatic Stress Disorder (PTSD), a condition first attributed to the trauma of warfare in the 1980s. More recently, Complex PTSD (C-PTSD) was found to affect victims of traumatic emotional injuries, such as those caused by sexual exploitation and domestic partner abuse.

According to the *Journal of Traumatic Stress*, C-PTSD results from the psychological impact of subordination to coercive control. It shares many common features with violently induced PTSD. Coercive control exists in all forms of domestic abuse, whether violent or non-violent, and can include manipulation through minimization, denial, lies, promises, excuses, rationalizations, blame, sexual abuse, reproductive coercion, and a host of additional behaviors.[6]

In PTSD, one event triggers a trauma reaction. But in C-PTSD, many separate instances of trauma pile up on the victim. C-PTSD is insidious. Some sexual hoaxes last a short time. Others continue unabated for an extended period of time. But when you learn the truth, you also discover that each intimate moment you shared was actually an act of defilement.

When emotionally abused, the victim may dismiss individual incidents because they're not life threatening or violent. But the accumulation of fear, defilement, or helplessness beats them down. When they discover that they've been sexually violated through deception, all of those undermining moments hit them all at once.

Romance scams can cause lost wages and even lead to physical illness. Victims can be plagued with trust issues for the rest of their lives. A person engaging in e-dating has a greater chance of being scammed than of contracting breast cancer, which is estimated at approximately 12% of the female population. In other words, romance scamming is psychologically and physically damaging. Aided by the internet, it has reached epidemic proportions!

So let's first deal with the 800-pound gorilla in the room. Much of society believes that people who get scammed are gullible, naïve, needy, or stupid. While those words could indeed describe some romance scam victims, even very smart, self-assured, independent people can be victimized. Scammers are practiced at the art of ripping people off, and they are good at what they do.

I recently spoke with a New Jersey senator's chief of staff about introducing a "catfish law" in his state. I was accompanied by a victim who'd been hoodwinked in a scam that began with a catfish profile on the e-dating site, "Plenty of Fish." Over a span of many months, the offender convinced the victim they were heading toward marriage as he emptied out her entire 401K savings account and left her with crippling credit card debt.

Beth, the victim, is an intelligent woman who runs a professional practice as a physical trainer. The offender had sold her a bill of goods similar to the Ponzi scheme committed by convicted felon, Bernie Madoff. He claimed to be an investment banker who could provide her with a greater return on her retirement account than her present wealth manager. He even had a sophisticated website to support those claims. He also told her he was divorced with one daughter. Instead, he was married with four children. She fell in love with him, and she trusted him.

The three of us — Beth, Al (the chief of staff), and I — spoke at length about the defilement victims feel when they're defrauded of sexual consent. He posed just about every objection I'd heard in the many years I've advocated for sexual assault by fraud victims. He claimed he was doing so to play "Devil's Advocate."

At one point, I turned to Beth and asked, "Of everything that's happened to you, the loss of your money, your ongoing debt, and the unwanted sexual violation, which has had the most profound effect on you?"

"His sexual assault," Beth said, without a moment of hesitation.

"I can understand how you feel," Al said, and then he turned my way. Looking directly at me, as if Beth were no longer in the room, he continued; "But the one thing I just can't wrap my head around is, aren't these women just gullible?"

I was astounded. I didn't want to cause Beth any further embarrassment than she already had faced. But the following day, I sent Al a note stating, "Even if the person is gullible to the greatest extent possible, no one deserves being sexually exploited. Being gullible is not a crime. Sexually assaulting someone is."

Lying and deceit are not new; they've been with us since the beginning of man. Even prehistoric animals used devices and trickery to attract other wildlife or avoid being caught by predators. The ability to change color or shape is built into the DNA of many species; chameleons, for example, change their outward appearance to suit their needs. Unfortunately, a person's DNA, mixed with their values, can generate the ability to shift personality and identity. Scientists have recently begun to explore the role brain chemistry plays in our character and decision-making processes.

Attraction causes dopamine levels to rise in the brain. Dopamine, in turn, initiates the flow of serotonin, oxytocin, and other hormonal activity. Oxytocin, a neuropeptide, is secreted into the bloodstream by the pituitary and influences the creation of bonding and trust. Oxytocin is currently undergoing study by researchers and universities around the world.

Catfish profilers are savvy about raising hormone and neuropeptide levels in people they target in order to stimulate the emotions fueled by brain chemistry. While offenders might not recognize that there is actual science behind their strategies, they instinctively comprehend the "laws of attraction" and manipulate people with ease.

Internet dating puts catfish in close proximity to a pool that's brimming with readily accessible prey. Finding a love interest is as easy as dropping their hooks into the well-stocked waters of a salmon farm. They simply have to choose which fish to reel in. They can remake themselves in the image of anyone they wish, based on the interests of their targets.

Misusing romantic brain chemistry creates easy access to sex, assets, and even immigration status. But the motives behind catfishing don't stop there. Sometimes catfish are simply bored. They may be looking for revenge or hoping to satisfy unrequited feelings of love. Their motivations are individual and endless.

When we place our profiles on a dating site or social

network, we're exposing ourselves to the unknown. While there may be honest people who meet our interests, there are others with morality issues who'll abuse information we've supplied to secure their own underhanded objectives.

Modern mental health professionals tell us that up to approximately 13% of the world population is made up of character-disordered people — individuals with flawed morality. Here's how the numbers break down according to the *Diagnostic and Statistical Manual of Mental Disorders (DSM)*, published by the American Psychiatric Association (APA). As many as

- 3.3% have Anti-Social Personality Disorder
- 1.8% have Borderline Personality Disorder
- 6.2% have Narcissistic Personality Disorder
- 1.8% have Histrionic Personality Disorder

Together they comprise what are widely known as Cluster B Personality Disorders. Individuals who have these disorders are referred to as *narcissists, sociopaths,* and *psychopaths.* Criminologists use the concept of a "dark triad" of morality disorders, which includes narcissism, Machiavellianism (malignant narcissism), and psychopathy.

Noted Irish psychotherapist, Christine Louis de Canonville, draws on her considerable background in forensics and criminology to instruct psychologists, psychiatrists, and mental health practitioners on treatment for the condition she refers to as Narcissistic Victim Syndrome (NVS). She believes that narcissism is growing significantly and has already reached "pandemic" proportions.

Dr. de Canonville wrote her book, *The Three Faces of Evil,* in order to make the distinction between various types of character disorders. But since the technical differences between these malfunctions do not significantly change the outcomes for their victims, and in an effort to focus on the issue of the crimes they commit, I'll stick with the generic term, *sociopath,* for the balance of this discussion.

Here's some disturbing news: if you're in a room with twenty-five other people, there could be as many as three *sociopaths* in your midst. And if you're a kindhearted person, they are much more likely to spot you — long before you could identify them. The exception to this rule is *histrionics,* people with histrionic personality disorder. Histrionics are often good-looking; they consistently strive to be the center of attention and are prone to emotional outbursts. Their character makes them a bit more obvious to spot once you know what you're looking for. Generally, however, there's unlikely to be anything disturbing in a morally disordered person's appearance to give them away.

In the internet world, a sociopath can and will create multiple profiles and register their information on numerous sites. You can't be certain of the real identity of the person behind the data, or even the validity of their photo. The photograph could be of a much younger version of themselves, or it may be a different person entirely. Even determining whether they're a man or a woman is impossible, as a victim in a 2015 case in the UK learned the hard way. She fell prey to Gayle Newland, a woman who passed herself off as a man.

Newland and the victim met through Facebook. She claimed to have physical deformities that resulted from illness and feigned deep-rooted insecurity about her (his) appearance. She convinced the victim to wear a blindfold during intercourse in order to spare her embarrassment. In the 10 times the couple engaged in sex, Newland used a prosthetic device to penetrate her unknowing victim. The woman, who was heterosexual, was thoroughly devastated when she learned she'd had sex with another woman. The jury found Newland guilty of sexual assault by fraud, and she was sentenced to an eight-year jail term.

Internet profiles can be patently false, entirely true, or somewhere in between. To the reader, their level of truth is unknown. In a coming chapter, we'll discuss tips to put the odds of discovery in your favor.

Our species, homo sapiens, is built to bond. In fact, isolating someone from society is considered a hostile act, even in prison populations. Isolation is so detrimental to a person's psyche that it's used as a form of torture. In its 2015 report, *Boxed In,* the New York Civil Liberties Union reported that 34% of the suicides in New York State's prison system took place while inmates were held in extreme isolation, yet less than 10% of all their inmates were held that way.[7]

We all want to socialize, love, and be loved (unless we possess the traits of a Cluster B personality disorder, that is). That desire puts us at high risk for encountering a catfish profiler when we use the internet as a resource. Our brain chemistry arouses our bonding, love, and trust impulses into action as a result of words, attention, and affection, even when the person they came from is sight unseen. Our thought process forms an image of who they are, inspired by their false information.

In his highly acclaimed book, *The Moral Molecule,* Dr. Paul Zak describes the importance of oxytocin in fueling the emotions that couple us with our loved ones, and even our pets. Recent studies have shown that gazing into the eyes of our canine buddies causes them to feel a sense of belonging, and vice versa.

Sarah Knapton of the London Daily Telegraph[8] reported on experiments conducted by the University of Tokyo and Duke University that tested the oxytocin effects of touching, talking to, and gazing at our pet dogs. These studies concluded that this interaction between the species drove up the levels of oxytocin found in the urine of each.

"These results suggest that humans may feel affection for their companion dogs similar to that felt toward human family members," said Dr. Miho Nagasawa, a researcher in the Department of Animal Science at Azabu University in Sagamihara, Japan. Dr. Nagasawa also reported that oxytocin factors heavily in regulating social bonding between mothers and their infants, as well as between sexual partners.[9]

People in the Cluster B category have been adversely impacted by their DNA, their development, or a combination of both, rendering them void of the ability to develop a conscience or bond out of love. Their brain structures and brain chemistry are faulty. This malfunction is a lifelong condition; a disorder, not an illness. Treatment is not altogether impossible — depending on the severity and source of the problem.

Intervention might improve their behavior — but it's unlikely to fix their basic sense of morality.

In most cases, treatment only enables the sociopath to fit more easily into society so they're less noticeable as they wreak havoc on everyone around them. "Cluster Bs" don't think there is anything wrong with them. Instead, it's the rest of the world that has the problems. They're resistant to seeking help and generally only do so when it's required, such as when a judge rules that they must.

Without normal bonding mechanisms, people can couple, but only out of need or want, not out of love. Their emotions are shallow, only as deep as their needs, and their mindset is "What's in it for me?" When their wants are satisfied or change, bonding will cease, unless another self-serving desire arises.

How and Why People Become Scammers

The specific character traits missing from the minds of sociopaths are emotional and compassionate empathy. If the sociopath's brain lacks the building blocks for it, empathy simply can't form. And, as a result, conscience can't form.

Conversely, people with high levels of emotional empathy may be more vulnerable and forgiving than people who have a lesser degree. They are inclined to feel trust, forgiveness, and compassion toward their fellow man. And unless they are enlightened about how a sociopath's brain operates, they project their own level of kindness and sensitivity onto others. They have difficulty grasping that someone who seems to love them, who has built a trusting bond with them, could be a total fraud. Their brain chemistry and moral code will cause them to remain committed and forgive.

Mental health professionals like Dr. Daniel Goleman, who wrote *Three Kinds of Empathy,* have gone to great lengths to explain the empathy phenomenon. What follows is an overview of its impacts.

Emotional Empathy — Feeling another person's emotions

Emotional empathy is the knee-jerk reaction we experience when someone near us falls off a chair or is otherwise injured. Without emotional empathy, you would not sense a kindred connection to their condition. That innate, emotional link is what prevents people from wishing harm on another human being.

Emotional empathy enables us to embrace another person's feelings as if we were sharing their experience. Relating to their pain inhibits our desire to cause them harm, which is the condition we refer to as "having a conscience." When we lack empathy, we may know the difference between wrong and right, but if harming someone else gets us our objective, only fear of exposure or consequences will curb our behavior.

A person without conscience is expected to obey society's rules and laws, even if they don't relate to them. They can and will appear appropriately behaved when their upbringing has exposed them to a code of conduct consistent with law-abiding society. But fear of exposure or consequences, not meaningful concern, is the driving force that inhibits their bad behavior. They can emulate conscience even though they don't have one, but they can harm people at will without the pangs of guilt or remorse that a morally intact person would experience. As long as they think they won't be found out, they will do whatever it takes to get what they want.

People with appropriate levels of empathy go through life thinking that everyone has it...until they discover they've stumbled into the path of a sociopath. Even then, recognition comes slowly, and with great turmoil. How could someone who demonstrated such caring toward them have no real emotional bond? While the empath provided love and concern, the other person was simply draining them for whatever benefits they were after.

To quickly summarize, Catfish profilers take on any character they choose to get you hooked. They design their online profiles to draw you in based on the laws of attraction, and then they stir up your sense of attachment and deprive you of anything they want. Because of their character flaws, their ends justify their means.

Morally intact people see bad behavior as *mistakes,* and they're willing to forgive. They extend the same courtesies to others that they would want themselves. They'll tolerate high levels of incongruity without suspicion. A person without conscience sees that mindset as the perfect opportunity. To them, empathy and caring are weaknesses rather than the "highest form of humanity" that they are.

Without the bounds of conscience, sociopaths can compete ruthlessly and are often extremely successful in business. Even in social situations, politics, and sports, not having the compassion that stems from emotional empathy can drive high levels of achievement. In our success-rewarded society, it's not unusual to find sociopaths at the top of social or business ladders.

Often, people with Cluster B personalities — sociopaths — are drawn to politics. Three high ranking officials in one state were recently convicted of serious crimes; one for eight counts of federal corruption including bribery and extortion, another for pressuring a real estate developer who had business before the Assembly into making inappropriate payments to his son. The last resigned in shame due to a scandal over his involvement with a prostitute. All of their crimes were carried out over an extended period of time. A sense of being "above the law" is typical of people who lack emotional empathy and fall within the bounds of Cluster B.

The correlation between sociopaths and empathetic, emotionally intact people easily compares to the relationship between wolves and dogs. Although they're both canines, a wolf is a predator, while a dog could unequivocally be your best friend.

Man has lived in partnership with dogs through the ages by taming their behavior and breeding away their aggression. The fable of the wolf in sheep's clothing has represented our image of the cunning predator whose passive exterior hides their sinister interior. But shepherds are often aided in rounding up their flock by their faithful dogs.

Wolves have a distinct physical appearance that sets them apart from dogs, while sociopaths have no specific visible traits to distinguish them from responsible, moral members of society. Unfortunately, they don't breathe fire out of their armpits, which would make them a lot easier to spot. They're as individual as any other human being. On the internet, they're even more  difficult to identify, since you can't see their facial cues or hear the tone of their voice. Their ability to interact with you and raise your level of attraction, before you even meet, makes them especially dangerous.

Cognitive Empathy — Sensing what's going on around us

Cognitive empathy enables us to perceive what's happening with our neighbors. Just because you know what they're experiencing and what motivates them, however, does not mean you'll exhibit caring or be able to put yourself in their shoes. In fact, with sociopaths, cognitive empathy accomplishes the opposite.

Strong cognitive empathy is a tool torturers rely on to shake down a prisoner for information. They can detach completely from any sense of pathos toward their victim. People who have high levels of cognitive empathy are frequently found in politics, sales, or police work. They're adept at figuring out what makes you tick. When directed in a positive way, cognitive empathy is extremely valuable and helpful. But having elevated levels of cognitive empathy and low levels of emotional empathy can be a lethal mix.

Vetting candidates for police work should include determining the candidate's depth of emotional and cognitive empathy so that a gun and badge don't fall into the wrong hands. Sociopaths crave excitement due to their inherent nature. Thus, they are frequently drawn to hazardous work, and positions of authority. Establishing a high bar for morality testing could help weed-out individuals who might be prone to committing police brutality.

Sociopaths are intuitive about the needs and wants of their targets. They'll use cognitive clues to create an image that will be readily accepted. Looking at your internet profile gives them all the information they need to begin the process of catching and scamming you.

Just like a chameleon changes colors, they'll adjust their behavior. Most people who recover from relationships with sociopaths think back on them as "reptiles" for good reason. There is a distinct cold-bloodedness in the way they operate. Having cognitive empathy and no conscience enables sociopaths to become swindlers like convicted conman, Bernie Madoff.

Compassionate Empathy — How we make a difference in people's lives

A person with high levels of emotional empathy might be hamstrung in an emergency because they'd be too upset to react appropriately. That's where *compassionate empathy* kicks in. Through compassionate empathy, we can use our emotional and cognitive skills to produce a meaningful result.

- Cognitive empathy tells us about people we share the universe with.
- Emotional empathy makes us care what happens to them.
- Compassionate empathy enables us to come to their aid when there's a problem.

A person with a well-balanced level of compassionate empathy will help an individual in peril, calling 911 if needed or figuring out what the situation calls for. They'll appear outwardly cool in a pinch, even while feeling significant concern for the person who's in danger. While they might fall apart after the crisis ends, they'll remain sufficiently detached to provide assistance when it's needed.

In the ABC television show, *What Would You Do?*, host John Quinones stages problematic social situations while his crew catches the reactions of onlookers on hidden cameras. Many of those witnessing these uncomfortable situations take no interest or refuse to get involved. Others are quick to come to the aid of the person in trouble. The do-gooders are likely to be motivated by their compassionate empathy.

Catfish profilers who are not driven by conscience have no qualms about how their lying will harm you. The internet provides them with a veil of anonymity and access through which they can locate and fool other participants. In order to engage safely in e-dating, one must recognize that not everyone is operating with a moral compass. It's best to thoroughly check the background of the people you meet.

If you're a person who believes that everyone is basically good, just misunderstood, and that your love and tolerance can overcome the personality flaws of others, I apologize for bursting your bubble. The only thing you'll ever change about a sociopath is their motivation, but not their morality. They are capable of behaving in a socially acceptable fashion, but only when it gets them what they want.

Baiting the Hook: How We Get Reeled In

T he desire to be loved is a driving force for people with emotional and compassionate empathy, but that interest puts us at risk of becoming embroiled in a toxic romance. Our empathy is at the heart of the forgiveness we extend to others and the tolerance that a catfish can prey on.

Unfortunately, sociopaths have an almost radar-like ability when it comes to identifying who to target. With detective-like precision, they seem able to sniff out a person's empathy from across a crowded room. They'll begin the "grooming" process by engaging you, testing their reading of you, and feeling out what will work on you. They're

attentive listeners, and you'll feel an instantaneous connection with them. Their glibness can cover a multitude of sins as they zero in on what's important to you.

Your empathy is evident in how you speak — politely deferring to others and providing a normal give-and-take during discussions. Conversations about past experiences and values reveal even more information about your personal level of empathy and forgiveness. We give away clues about ourselves not only when we're face-to-face, but also through internet exchanges. A catfish scammer can use a multitude of grooming tricks to bring you under their control.

Love-Bombing

To build trust and fuel a sense of belonging, catfish prime their intended marks with an overabundance of loving gestures, interest, gifts, attention, and commitments. Doing so stirs the *laws of attraction* hormones into motion. And nothing does so better than sex.

Their target will feel an immediate bond, as if they've found their soulmate. And though modern society no longer considers sex before marriage to be taboo, people who rush into sexual hookups with someone they meet on the internet put themselves at risk for being swindled by false love.

Mirroring

Sociopaths will become the opposite-sex version of you (or same-sex version in gay coupling.) Their values and interests will seem to mirror yours, and they'll agree with your philosophy in 'most everything you discuss. In short order, your connection will feel intense.

Favors as a means of attachment

A catfish might dangle a small request for a token favor. They're testing to determine how accommodating their target is. Compassionate empathy will motivate a positive response. Establishing small and sometimes reciprocal favors will encourage even deeper trust. The same device is used by pedophiles to deceive children. It's the "Can you help me find my lost puppy?" ploy. Skilled sociopaths successfully apply this technique to manipulate adults. We tend to feel a bond with a person we've helped. Performing a favor for someone strengthens our attachment to them.

Jiggling the hook

The contrary works as well. If the fisherman draws his hook away from his intended prey, he'll often cause a fierce grab at the bait. Pulling you in and then pushing you away will quickly establish the scammer's goal of attachment. They may begin the romance by cancelling on you at first, with "good reason," of course! They may explain their aloofness with an excuse like being wary because of a prior relationship, the *pity-ploy*. They're actually grooming you through the game of *push-pull*.

Instilling fear

Catfish are known to plant seeds that ultimately can be used to intimidate and silence their victims. One such example is to suggest taking intimate photos in compromising poses. Ultimately, the victim could become coerced into silence by the threat of those photos getting posted on the internet for the world to see.

Dr. Emma Short, a researcher and lecturer at the University of Bedfordshire, has drawn attention to this problem both in the US and the UK. She states, *"[Because] non-consensual porn so often involves the internet and social media, the public and the law [have] sometimes struggled to understand the mechanics of the conduct and the devastation it can cause. Although revenge porn can happen in a number of contexts, such as broken friendships or for financial gain from an unknown third party, frequently, the intimate images are themselves the result of an abuser's coercion of a reluctant partner."*[10]

A woman I'll call Linda related that the "man of her dreams" convinced her to take intimate pictures. "You would have quite the presence on the internet," he said as he chuckled and snapped his camera.

His reasoning behind taking the photos was that he wanted to see her when they were apart. "I don't want to look at another woman, only you," he claimed. Over a year later, when she recognized how badly she'd been conned, she also realized that his joking had been a deliberate attempt to silence her should she ultimately learn the truth.

Linda wanted justice, but those intimate photos were still out there. Ultimately, her interest in stopping him from harming others won out, and she bravely filed legal action against him.

At the time of this writing, the case is still pending in Florida.

In July, 2016, California Congresswoman Jackie Speier introduced a US federal law to prevent revenge porn. Thirty-four states have already enacted such laws. If passed, the federal law will close the gap for the balance of the nation.

Another method of intimidation predators use is to tell stories about how tough they are. They might even show you a weapon or relate an incident in which they harmed another person. While you may think they're trying to build a bond by confiding in you, they're really making sure you're adequately silenced by fear when you figure them out.

Once they're convinced the victim is sufficiently snagged, the catfish will spring their mega-request, and it's often for money, deviant sex acts, or immigration support. Sex addicts account for a high volume of catfish activity. They usually juggle more than one fish on their line, and they are constantly trolling for more.

Depending on what they're really after, a catfish's appeal for money might look like an emergency — an immediate need for medical treatment, for instance, or steps to avoid deportation. Sexual exploitation could begin as a request to "prove your love." Targets who fail to fork over the goods will be hit with shaming or a scathing attack aimed at undermining their self-esteem. Righteous indignation is often a character disordered sham to manipulate a person with a loving, caring mentality when they don't readily comply with a demand.

Even once they realize they've been harmed, victims are often too embarrassed, confused, or afraid to immediately seek help. When they do, the police rarely act if the assailant is known by the victim. And they tend to overlook crimes that are not violent.

Sociopaths don't stick around when people get wise to them. They get out and frequently "gaslight" (cause the victim to doubt their own sanity). They'll hurl blame at the injured party for the relationship's end or otherwise defame them to onlookers. They spin around so many of the details that the victim begins to question their own sense of reality. Often family and friends in the victim's close support group are equally fooled by the offender and may not see through the manipulation they're witnessing.

Lauren's Story

"Carlos Lamborghini" is not the name of the man who snagged Lauren Lazarro of Tampa Bay FL. I've changed his name to protect the victim. But he's a catfish whose name is not his only resemblance to a speedy Italian sports car.... He can rip a woman off in zero to ten seconds!

Lauren tried to locate a romantic partner through online dating. The fact that she's an educated, intelligent medical professional didn't protect her from Carlos's charms. Here's what happened, in her own words:

"I was defrauded on a popular dating site by a complete impostor presenting himself as a wealthy, romantic, Italian man who had been a cruise ship officer and presently worked as a marketing

entrepreneur. He was charming and suave. All of his professionally designed web pages and online credentials, including video endorsements from several sources, supported his claims.

I fell in love with him. He successfully employed push-pull tactics to get me hooked. He cancelled the first date at the last minute and, two weeks into our whirlwind relationship, he announced sudden business-related plans to move away. After that, our contact was conducted long-distance with occasional romantic getaways.

He called every night at 10 p.m. I set an individual ring for him on my phone and looked forward to hearing it every evening. Its absence created a cavernous hole to remind me of my loss once I learned what he was actually doing.

He defrauded me of thousands of dollars and over a year of my life. He tried to come after a lot more money to finish me off. He lied about entrepreneurial successes, his age, and his marital status. While he'd made promises of a wonderful future together, including marriage and 'seeing the world,' he had a wife waiting for him at home.

Without legislation on the use of 'false personation' to conduct rape by fraud, I can't even file a complaint with the sheriff's office. I was told, 'Lesson learned,' and 'Don't come back!' So, the problem is that this predator can set up shop in town with internet dating, scam a lot of women in a local area, and then flee the area. I am sure there are more victims of this man in Florida. It was an elaborate scheme."

Lamborghini groomed Lauren by keeping his initial requests for money small. He used the pity-ploy of "medical expenses." He had succeeded in priming the pump. Over a fourteen-month period, he felt confident he'd created a large enough trust base to go for the big kill. He asked Lauren for $65K. When she declined, he berated her for refusing to help him and letting him down. Then he abruptly slithered away to con his next victim, leaving her utterly devastated.

Lauren was heartbroken and shocked about what had transpired. She grappled with a terrible sense of defilement. Once she began making progress on getting her self-esteem back together, she realized she needed to demand the return of her money. The police refused to intervene.

In all, Lamborghini had siphoned $16K from Lauren's pockets. He responded to her appeals for reimbursement with self-righteous indignation, claiming the moral high ground that her request was insulting and inappropriate. "People in serious relationships like ours take care of each other, don't they?" he said. He never once admitted that he had a wife of 25 years back home in California. There had never been what he'd claimed was a monogamous, committed relationship leading to marriage.

Lauren's subsequent research turned up Lamborghini's dark past of fleecing elderly victims for dancing lessons that never materialized. His entrepreneurial business claims had been smoke and mirrors. He'd created a well-orchestrated *catfish profile* to lure her in. And this independent, intelligent woman had swallowed the bait — hook, line, and sinker!

Even when violence occurs, if the victim has been *catfished*, the police rarely get involved. A woman I'll call Barbara met her love interest through "Plenty of Fish," one of the largest internet dating sites. After he brutally raped her, she attempted to report his violent sexual assault to the police in the small tourist town in Southern New Jersey where they lived. The policeman responded, "It's a 'he-said, she-said,'" and, "If you record him admitting what he did, we'll look into it." The officer completely ignored the physical evidence and never followed up with a possible witness to the incident. No investigation took place.

Removing the victim's rose-colored glasses is painful!

Coming to grips with the awareness that the person you thought you were dating is actually someone completely different is especially difficult when you've been defrauded of sex and love. Being deceived into sex is "sexual assault by fraud." Being deceived into love is "emotional rape." Often, both forms of harm go hand in hand.

Cutting deeply into a person's core intimacy causes massive loss of self-trust and pervasive depression. It took Lauren considerable soul searching and heartache to get back on her feet. No laws currently exist in Florida to stop Lamborghini from doing the same thing to his next victim.

Barbara not only needed therapy, she needed to move out of the state in order to escape her fears that she'd encounter her attacker around every corner. She frequently ran into him while driving in her community, and on several occasions, she noticed his car on her block. The authorities did nothing.

Were You Seduced, or Were You "Sexploited?" How Can You Tell?

Someone who lies in order to seduce you sees you as a prize, an entitlement, a piece of property — not as the living, breathing, caring human being that you are. They have no respect for your autonomy over your body and will contrive to overcome your resistance any way they can. They intellectually know wrong from right, but they think rules, laws, and common decency don't apply to them unless they get caught.

Sexual predators don't care whether you suffer harm or not. To them, your body is simply a means to their ends. The fact that you actually live inside it, and that no one has the right to touch your reproductive organs without your fully knowledgeable and informed agreement, *consent,* is irrelevant to them.

The penal codes of most states aid the predator. Instead of addressing the deeply harmful sexual exploitation (sexploitation) that takes place when they deceptively hook you, law enforcement won't even consider stepping in until you suffer hefty monetary losses. Even then, justice or restitution is difficult to achieve.

Assent and *consent* are similar but different under the law. And that difference makes scamming you for sex a crime. Assenting to an action indicates agreement, but assent does not necessarily mean that the person granting agreement is *fully cognizant* or *knowing* when they do so. Because being knowledgeable and informed are inherent elements in consent, the concept that consent can occur without the victim being "knowledgeable and informed" is an oxymoron.

When the offender deliberately lies, the victim is unaware that their decision is based on untruth. If someone has lied to you about their identity and personal characteristics, you cannot make an informed decision about sexual intimacy. You are not being seduced; you are being sexploited.

Your agreement was deliberately and treacherously clouded by the offender. They know they obtained your *uninformed* assent, but not your *informed* consent. And they also know they tricked you into thinking you were consenting when, indeed, you were not.

Outsiders act in bizarre ways when a victim complains about the contamination they feel from all forms of sexual assault, including catfish hooking. Many believe that if it doesn't violently harm you, you are not "hurt." They do not relate to the sense of defilement that engulfs your mind.

We might think we've come a long way from the days when women were told, "If rape is inevitable, go with it." But that's exactly what the close friend of a woman I'd advocated for said when she was violently raped.

"What's the big deal about rape?" the friend asked. "Just relax and enjoy it." The offender in this case — we'll call him Stuart — took advantage of the fact that the victim was so petrified that she vomited and passed out. She came to as he was raping her and snapping photos on his cell phone. When he finished, he dragged her by one foot across the garage floor and held her against her will overnight.

In his dating site profile, Stuart had lied about both his identity and the nature of the connection he wanted. He said he was seeking a committed, monogamous relationship. He was really seeking a "swinger" for hook-ups with other couples to satisfy his sex addiction. As I write, he's trolling for more unsuspecting sex partners on multiple sites even though he's fooled another victim into thinking their relationship is monogamous. He's asked her to marry him, engagement ring and all.

His new fiancé called the police recently when Stuart pulled her by her hair and tossed her down a flight of stairs. He was after a swinger hook-up with her as well, and she refused. She filed a criminal complaint and learned that two restraining orders had previously been issued against him. She also knew that his prior victim alleged that he'd violently raped her. Yet she returned to the relationship with this dangerous sociopath and withdrew the criminal charge she'd filed.

People often wonder why victims continue in toxic relationships. I'll be dealing with the reasoning behind this seemingly irrational behavior in the next chapter.

When and why a catfish's *sexploitation* is a crime

People think of online dating profiles as personal advertising. We all expect puffery in how goods and services are sold. But no other forms of false advertising, not even criminally prosecuted *bait-and-switch tactics,* infringe on our self-determination over our reproductive organs.

Bait-and-switch scams can result in criminal penalties and civil litigation, even when the victim knew full well that the product they purchased differed from the ad that attracted them. Bait-and-switch allows you to file a civil claim because the offender's actions deprived you of assets. Many sexually snagged victims need ongoing therapy to recover their wellbeing. A non-consensual sexual act was committed against their person. Yet most states fail to provide victims with any means of relief or validity.

The victim does not discover the truth until well after they were sexploited. But not recognizing your loss or the harm committed until after the fact does not excuse the behavior. No act of fraud is recognized as it transpires.

Before engaging in sex, people who've lied should clear up their deceptions and false information. It's one thing to attract a person with lies. It's heartless, mean and underhanded to do so, but not a crime. It's quite another to violate their reproductive organs by lying.

Check ID!

Before you even consider having sex with someone you meet on the internet, please, please PLEEAASSE... check them out thoroughly, including asking for their photo ID! Be sure their details support everything they've said. Giving you a fictitious name is a deliberate attempt to hide material facts about who they are. It makes discovery all but impossible. Don't be sexually intimate with anyone until you feel emotionally intimate enough to ask the hard questions and secure proof of what they've told you.

Don't wait 'til you're hopping into bed with them to ask. Be well aware of who they are long before you get to that point. And remember what righteous indignation signals! If they're insulted by your request, they either don't care about whether or not you feel safe, or they have something to hide. In either case, you're better off knowing BEFORE you become intimate with them. Resistance to providing credible, verifiable information like a driver's license is a red flag. Chances are good that they're married, older or younger than they've claimed, or hiding other significant information.

Because sociopaths look like the person next door, spotting them takes a watchful, knowledgeable eye. It's difficult to view people realistically as they're pouring on the charm that stirs up your romantic brain chemistry! But until you're well acquainted with their values and their ID, remain emotionally detached.

Recognizing a catfish

Check out all potential suitors through internet resources — no exceptions! BeenVerified, Jail.com, TrueLoveScams.com, LiarsCheatersRUS.com, and RomanceScamsNow.com are just a few of many sites that post offenders. Make note of the license plate number for their car. Conducting a motor vehicle search could uncover a fictitious name. Look into their friends'  backgrounds as well. Had Lauren done so, she would have known that Carlos Lamborghini's "business associates" were convicted felons.

Mental health professionals have drawn a strong correlation between high testosterone levels and low oxytocin. That's not to say that all world-class athletes are sociopaths, but we should not be surprised at the amount of sexual and domestic abuse in the news involving high-profile sports figures.

Joe Paterno, the Head Coach of Penn State's Nittany Lions, played quarterback for Brown University. While he claimed he knew nothing of the sexual assaults committed by Penn State's Defensive Coach, Jerry Sandusky, testimony was released in July 2016, saying he'd known about Sandusky's behavior since 1976. Assault victim, John Doe #150, testified that he complained to Paterno who responded, "I don't want to hear about any of that kind of stuff; I have a football season to worry about."

Brock Turner, a star swimmer at Stanford University, was convicted of sexual assault against an unconscious woman.

His father, Dan Turner, made headlines by characterizing his son's behavior as "20 minutes of action," when he pleaded for probation for his son. The judge, Aaron Persky, seemed more concerned with the rapist's future than the horror the victim will be plagued with for a lifetime. Of a possible 14 year sentence, he sent Turner to jail for six months. Turner only served three months before his release.

Here are clues that could signal you're being charmed by a catfish:

- *They neither Skype nor phone.*

    There's always a plausible reason: They aren't good with technology. The dog ate their phone. They loaned it to their child. Their system doesn't support the software. In this day and age, if someone is serious about e-dating, they'll get the necessary equipment to communicate in an above-board, transparent fashion. Online messenger chats are often the communication tool catfish prefer. It's a huge red flag!

- *They try to quickly move your conversation away from the service that introduced you.*

    They want your distinct contact information. Also, the messages you exchange through the site where you met can be traced and reviewed. They want their correspondence separated from discovery or oversight as quickly as possible.

- *You've met and are building a relationship, but they hide you from their family or friends.*

    It's possible their friends and family don't live nearby, but do they have any contact? Are you included in the conversations they conduct? Someone who truly cares about you will be proud to have you meet the other loved ones in their life. Hiding you from their friends could indicate that they don't want you hearing the truth that someone who knows them may pass along.

- *They conduct their conversations with you in secrecy.*

    If you speak to them on Skype, are there other people or human noises in the background? Catfish seek out privacy to conduct their conversations. If they speak in hushed tones and there are never any other people around, something's very fishy.

- *They establish a consistent time for you to communicate with them.*

    Ever tried to juggle? Catfish often scam more than one person at a time, and they have to keep your details separate from the rest. It's easier to juggle you on a schedule. A specific time may work best for them because their significant other is not around. They could also want easy access to you without having to chase you down. In Lauren's case, Lamborghini established a Pavlovian response that drew her back to him each night at 10 p.m. After she discovered the truth, the void she felt at that hour plagued her for many months to come.

- *They call you by a pet name in short order.*

    Honey, Baby, Sweetie, Beautiful. Yup, we all like to hear those private terms of endearment that make us feel special. Although they stir our brain chemistry, coming from a catfish, these names are a convenient way to avoid confusing you with other conquests.

- *Their family members warn you about them.*

    Sometimes people who've known them for years can be wrong about them, but they can also be painfully right. When a family member sticks out their neck to warn you, you should give the warning some serious consideration.

- *They don't seem to have any friends.*

    Even if they've moved to a new location, they should still be able to maintain prior relationships that they valued.

- *You don't like their friends.*

    Birds of a feather flock together. Beware.

- *They are highly critical of others.*

    Narcissists will try to build themselves up by bringing others down. They look for your faults. They don't forgive, but they expect you to forgive them. Catfish are often narcissists.

- *You discover a lie about any identity characteristic.*

    If they told you one lie, they've likely told you several. They'll take on any false persona they believe will hook you. You are not a real person to them; you are the prize in their con game.

- *They treat service people poorly.*

    Their inability to feel empathy often shows up in how they behave toward others, particularly if the person has little authority or is subservient to them, like a waiter or a valet.

- *They have an overblown self-image.*

  They'll talk a good game about their past, but you won't see evidence of the abilities they claim. There are incongruities: they have a high-profile job, for instance, but they are borrowing money from you. It's often difficult to get them to be forthcoming about business activities. Their responses may be vague, confusing, or unrealistic.

- *Watch their grammar and punctuation.*

  Their written language skills don't measure up to the level of education they claim. This incongruity is often present in the scams that come from Nigeria or other countries that are notorious for online scamming. Often, they'll fail to capitalize "I" or they'll confuse how to use the letter "s" in possessives vs. plurals

- *They don't follow through on plans.*

  They'll make promises but not live up to them. You'll get a lot of excuses and the smokescreen of confusion. Once is a mistake. Twice is a pattern. The third time… hit the delete key, hard!

- *They don't pay their way.*

  They forgot their wallet or lost their credit card. And it's happened more than once.

- *They travel… a lot.*

  Being "out of town" is a great cover for a person who's married or has multiple relationships. Many catfish scams are conducted as long-distance romances. Victims are often fooled by profiles claiming to be a soldier stationed in a war zone. It's a perfect cover for establishing a set time for communication and builds an instant image of someone who is dedicated, strong, and trustworthy.

- ***They don't discuss their children or their parents, or they speak ill of them.***

    Emotionally intact people have strong connections with their families. They feel pride and love toward them. Beware of claims they make when circumstances have pulled those relationships apart.

- ***They've never done a lick of volunteer work.***

    It's a pretty good sign that a person doesn't really care about society if they reach adulthood without feeling motivated to give back. They may even feign involvement with a charity to make themselves seem responsible and kindhearted. Donating money to causes is both helpful and tax deductible. Doing so may or may not reflect a person's true character.

- ***They're glib, charming, and sweep you off your feet.***

    Catfish, who are often sociopaths, may have an outstanding gift of gab. They can literally charm the pants off of you! They're adept at creating an instantaneous bond.

- ***They don't trust you and want you to "prove" yourself to them.***

    Unwarranted lack of trust rarely means that they were hurt, although caring people frequently misinterpret it as such. Loving people will often take pity on a person who seems unable to trust, but it can mean that they simply lack the "trust molecule," oxytocin — and a conscience.

- *They invade your privacy.*

    Prying into your emails, texts, or phone messages can signal lack of trust and a controlling mentality. They may peer over your shoulder when you input your password or disarm your security alarm. Be sure to keep your private codes to yourself.

- *They're immediately seductive and quickly feel like your soulmate.*

    Beware of people who are quick to touch you or create warm eye contact when they've just met you. Catfish are in a hurry to cast a physical spell without getting to know you. While they stir your brain chemistry to bond, there is no substance to the relationship. Victims with high levels of oxytocin will feel stimulated by their advances. Know your level of physical attraction to be sure you're not being *played* instead of being loved. If it feels too good to be true, it probably is.

- *They have a criminal past.*

    Yes, people make mistakes, but a criminal who is a sociopath will not change their stripes. They are who they are.

- *They don't financially support their children.*

    Regardless of what transpired between husband and wife, a non-custodial parent who does not send money to support their kids is irresponsible. They think of their children as pawns in a vicious game of control, not people.

- *Nothing is ever their fault.*

    Catfish will paint themselves as perpetual victims. Every bad thing that happened in their life was someone else's fault.

Checking photos and information on the internet

Using Google Reverse Image Search can uncover whether their posted photo is one that belongs to another person or is used elsewhere. Look up the tutorial for your browser online. You can also see the past dates an image was posted and get a clue regarding whether it's recent or not.

Predators who use old or other people's photos cannot comply with a request for a specific, current picture of them. Let's say you have a discussion about their pet dog or their view of the river from their living room. Ask them to take a *selfie* including the item you've discussed. Instead of emailing it to you, ask them to post it on their e-dating profile. If they disappear faster than you can say "catfish," you'll know what they are.

Catfish relationships will end with you feeling discarded

A catfish will use every trick in the book to hook you. They'll play you until you're wise to them and as long as they're getting what they want. When you become too curious or suspicious, they'll dump you and reel in the new fish they've hooked on their line.

Many of them don't even wait until you've figured them out. Instead, they juggle multiple victims all at once, like the New Jersey man who called himself Tom Gatto; he was married to two women and in relationships with several others. One of the women was even a dating coach!

He'd lied to each of them about his service record as a Marine and his credentials as a licensed practicing psychologist, and he'd convinced people he had terminal cancer. His degrees were forged. He'd never served in the military. All of his claims were bogus.

Debunking the Heart Myth

The concept that love resides in your heart is beautiful, isn't it? Unfortunately, it's not really true. Love is a brain function. If your heart stops, your brain will cease, but that's about the only link between your heart and love.

One of the most popular songs of 1959, *Love Potion #9,* was written by Lieber and Stoller and originally recorded by The Clovers. Although it's a spoof on a chemical concoction that makes people fall in love, it's not far from reality.

Romantic love has recently been shown to be a chemical addiction, creating hormonal responses similar to those triggered by drugs or alcohol. Serotonin, dopamine, oxytocin, vasopressin and other neuropeptides and hormones in our brains work together to attract us to others and establish and maintain loving bonds.[11]

This chemical concoction is intentionally powerful to enable our species to remain coupled throughout our children's

development. Because our offspring are among the slowest mammals to mature on the planet, our coupling chemistry is decidedly tough and resilient.

In addition, our amygdala and our frontal and prefrontal cortices all contribute to our facility to use judgment, apply analysis, and predict outcomes. The capacity of these neurological regions is diminished by the chemistry of romantic love, making it difficult to properly react when the relationship causes us trouble.

Our ability to feel unconditional love, the love of forgiveness, results from the strong clutches of our brain chemistry. For some people, even when they're betrayed or abused, their sense of attachment to their loved one does not come crashing down, though onlookers may think it should. The stronger their hormonal activity, the more difficult it becomes for them to break away.

Adding to the problem, the abrupt halt to the production of love chemicals, due to betrayal or violence, causes the release of stress hormones that can make us crave the romantic love we've lost. Instead of exiting the relationship, we become even more fiercely embedded in the bond. This phenomenon can also be strengthened by a condition known by several names; Betrayal Bond, Trauma Bond, and Stockholm Syndrome.

We frequently see relationship partners ignore all common sense to remain with abusive mates. Reeva Steenkamp, who was murdered by her lover, highly acclaimed South African

Paralympian, Oscar Pistorius, remained in the relationship despite several reports of intimidation and harm. The toxic glue of her brain chemistry caused her to forgive, trust, and hope for the best, instead of making a beeline for the closest exit. Her inability to respond to the red flags of danger ended tragically when Pistorius drilled four bullets through a closed bathroom door, killing her as she crouched helplessly beside the toilet.

If, instead of trying to "kick" the romance, the victim was an alcoholic attempting to abstain from alcohol, they'd experience intense cravings for a drink. And just like alcoholics should steer clear of bars if they want to recover, people who've been defrauded by romance scams should have no contact with their abuser in order to curb backsliding. The sight, sound, aroma, touch or even their own thoughts about their romantic partner can pull them right back into the toxic connection.

Society frequently puzzles over women who "stand by their man" through public exposure over their sexual wrongdoing. Some appear side-by-side with them during trials and press statements. Often the public ponders why these women seem to be selling out instead of admitting the obvious. The answer is simple, they're motivated by the toxic glue that drowns out rational thought and attaches them to their mate.

When we're bonded to a sociopath, what we believe to be a relationship is only a smokescreen they're using to hide their personal agenda. While we're experiencing love, our partner is using our emotion-charged brain chemistry for their personal gain. Their love is superficial and shallow at best. Catfish depend on the highly intoxicating nature of love and trust to rip people off. But sometimes, as was true in a recent case of con-meets-con, the tables can be turned on them.

Bob Rawlings probably selected his target, who I'll call Rebecca, because she worked in the health care field. Due to her occupation, it's likely he felt she would be an empathetic person.

Had Bob done his homework properly, he probably would have recognized that he stood a good chance of finding a "gold digger" at the site he used because its emphasis was to identify men of prominence. Characteristically, gold diggers are emotionally unavailable and seek wealth, fame, or to raise their status. Their emotional bonds are superficial. And they lack the conscience necessary to prevent them from hoodwinking others.

Once she knew she'd been conned, Rebecca arranged meetings with Bob where she carried a concealed camera and recorded their discussions. Then she lured him with charm into a meet-up she'd prearranged with the police. As they handcuffed him and escorted him to their squad car, the press she'd contacted stood by snapping pictures.

A woman in her circumstance with a high level of loving brain chemistry might be consumed by a betrayal bond or caught in the toxic glue of romance addiction. They'd struggle through feelings of attachment and experience bewildering mental states of love and hate at the same time. Instead, Rebecca callously planned and carried out the sting in which she conned a con artist.

A love that spanned continents

That wasn't the case for Suki. Her lover of two and a half years, Adam, a musician and producer for a major British network, traveled around the world on production assignments. She'd seen his Facebook profile, was attracted to him, and reached out.

Adam made her feel like they were truly in love. He convinced her he was waiting for his financial circumstances to change so they could be together permanently. They frequently expressed mutual devotion in texts, on video cam, and in phone calls. They pledged their love to each other during several rendezvous in London and New York City.

Adam mirrored Suki's values in order to build her trust. For example, when she tried to care for an abandoned kitten, he immediately responded with his tale of a similar rescue. He poured love and tenderness into their relationship as he artfully love-bombed her. After two and a half years, he abruptly called it quits. "It isn't practical," he informed her. Suki was devastated.

Her heart broken, Suki tried to figure out how Adam could be so committed one minute and "over it" the next. He'd professed profound love for her, building dreams of forever-after, and now he was gone. She began to search for the truth, and what she found shocked her.

Adam was married. His wife of 16 years was not the "ex-girlfriend" he "shared property with." They weren't "just friends," as he'd claimed. Indeed, he and his wife slept in the same bed, night after night, when he wasn't cavorting with other women all around the world. They had been together for a total of 25 years. He had a long history of betraying and manipulating his wife, yet she clung to the hope that he would stop.

An even darker side of Suki and Adam's relationship

emerged months later when she learned of another affair that existed alongside theirs. While they were enjoying a romantic visit in London, and while Suki thought they were engaged in monogamous sex, he texted another woman, characterizing Suki as an "ex-girlfriend who's dying." He claimed he was simply showing kindness toward her by "providing emotional support in her time of need." This revelation gouged an especially deep and painful gash in Suki's heart.

When the truth surfaced about his marriage, Suki confronted Adam. Like many catfish, he played the victim card. He lamented, "Everyone's upset at me," as if his behavior warranted something different. "I'm a disaster area," he claimed in an attempt to draw on her pity.

Adam neither apologized nor acknowledged his actions regarding the other woman. He was solely concerned about his "image" being tarnished and threatened Suki to prevent that from happening.

Suki struggled for months through deep depression that overwhelmed her ability to regain her self-esteem and feel "normal" again. Her reaction is typical of victims who discover they've been conned in a relationship hoax. They spend hour after hour ruminating about what they could have done differently to secure a better result. Even though they're angry at the betrayal, their emotional chemistry makes it difficult for them to turn off their feelings of love, and they juggle both emotions back and forth. Often, they wear out the patience of their friends and supporters, who believe they should simply "get over it."

Blame, Shame, and Recovery

Of the three most common goals of romance scams — for sex, for money, or for marriage/immigration status — the one that makes victims feel the most defiled is sexual exploitation. No matter what loss the victim sustains, they deserve the right to seek justice. Beth, the victim from chapter one who'd been catfished for both sex and assets worth over $200K, explained her pain this way:

"Now I will admit that in the past I would have probably blamed the victim too; we all pride ourselves on our ability to spot a con artist, a liar, a scumbag and smugly think 'that would never happen to me' — until it does. Then what was once pride turns to shame and embarrassment, and when you ask for help and are again shamed and embarrassed, that changes your self-worth and you become and remain a victim. Harmed forever.

There are no negative consequences for the perpetrator. We can call them con artists, but notice how we glorify it by using the word artist. It is time that people who lie, scheme, and mislead in the name of love are prosecuted; they have to be afraid of the consequences of their actions. They have to think twice before putting down an incorrect age, marital status, occupation, or picture on a profile. They need to understand that if they lie and manipulate to get something from someone (be it sex, money, etc.) that there are legal consequences. People who lie know that they are lying. They are lying for their own gain, and right now there are no legal ramifications for lying on a profile. Why does the honest person always have to look at the world through the dishonest person's eyes?"

Beth correctly portrays the lack of justice available to victims. The legal bills for going after her offender cost her over $50K, and he defaulted on the settlement they reached in civil court without making a single payment. He was a master at romantic persuasion and embroiled her in a sexual relationship that she *assented to*, but did not *consent to*, to raise her attachment and build her trust.

Back in the Roman era, Socrates pointed out the character-undermining quality of "sex by persuasion," which was his term for lying to induce sex. He remarked that violent rapists are obvious villains, but people who defraud for sex gouge the very character of the victim. And here's why...

In order for us to walk comfortably through the world, we need an element of trust. We must feel that the society around us means us no harm, and we take comfort from the thought that we can protect ourselves. If we did not feel this level of safety, we could not venture out of the door without a gun strapped on our hip.

Traumatic events destroy our trust. When we've been hurt by an external villain, we help protect ourselves by getting away from the place where we feel unsafe. But when we opened the door for the monster to walk through, the person we can't count on for protection is our very own self. We feel sexually violated by our judgment which diminishes our self-esteem. We become hypervigilant and plagued by anxiety.

We blame ourselves because we fail to recognize and acknowledge the highly specialized and refined ability of a scam artist to mess with our brain chemistry and pull off a decidedly believable hoax. And much of society fails to recognize just how cunning and duplicitous these criminals actually are.

The simple lie can be the most deceptive, but people also fall prey to totally ridiculous fabrications like the offender works for the British Defense Ministry or the FBI (which explains their need for secrecy or frequent travel). The less far-fetched the lie, however, the more believable it is.

What's the difference between violent assault and sexual harm by fraud?

No matter how we're sexually exploited, we feel violated at our very core. Victims of violent rape usually deal with a single incident of being defiled, and nothing can compare to the trauma of such an event. Violence is an overt act of aggression, while deception is a passive-aggressive, covert act of aggression.

In sexual assault by false personation, the victim is often violated over and over again. They've suffered an invasion of their reproductive organs that repulses them and makes them feel contaminated. They heap blame upon themselves for allowing the intrusion.

Did the victim want to be loved? Yes. Did they want to be lied to? No. They surrendered themselves to a character who existed only in their mind's eye, not to the actual *person* of the offender. In fact, the individual who exploited their reproductive organs was an unknown, a veritable stranger, who tricked them into trust in order to violate them. The victim simply did not know that a violation was happening at the time it took place.

Most people who fall prey to a sociopath have no idea of the likelihood of doing so. They don't suspect that sociopaths walk among us in polite society, pretending to be — and appearing — perfectly normal. They don't recognize that there's a huge number of sociopaths who troll e-dating and other internet sites to commit romance scams on multiple victims, or locate targets in other ways.

But shouldn't our gut instincts help us out?

Our *gut* responds to circumstances that are within our body of knowledge, understanding, and experience. Gut instincts will only protect us from things we're already aware of. Until now, society's recognition and awareness of emotional predators and the gross defilement of sexual assault by deception has been sketchy at best.

How do we regain our own self-trust?

First off, we have to have the will to do so. If you've been hurt by a sexual predator, it's likely that you see your life as an unsafe place. You may want to throw yourself into bed, pull the covers over your head, and curl up into a fetal position. You could want to remain withdrawn from society because you can't trust that you'll be safe in its midst. Lack of trust follows you like a shadow wherever you go, so you simply go nowhere and become reclusive.

In my efforts as an advocate, I often work with people as they struggle through this stage of recovery. Sadly, what victims often receive from people around them is condemnation, disempowerment, invalidation and blame. Ridding them of blame and shame is the first obstacle that must be overcome in order to restore their self-esteem.

People don't generally think they'll get snagged by a romance scam until it actually happens to them. Denigrating the victim as stupid or naïve keeps them drowning in their despair. And this type of invalidation causes them to relive the pain of the experience. Sexual assault of any kind deeply penetrates a victim's psyche. Expecting them to simply rise above their pain is an absurd expectation. In Lauren's words, "When you can view what happened to you as a crime, you can detach emotionally. It's very healing."

Until our legislators enact laws to bring scamming sexual predators to justice, many victims will not be as successful as Lauren was in escaping the pain of her ordeal. Instead, they'll be caught in the grip of shame and defilement for years to come. They'll suffer from C-PTSD, and the longer it persists, the more difficult their recovery becomes.

Swimming Free: Steps to Reclaim Your Self-Esteem and Your Life

Here are basic steps that can help victims breathe fresh air after being submerged in a toxic romance:

- ***Have NO CONTACT with the offender!***

    Yes, you'd like to tear their heart out! Yes you'd like an apology, at the very least. Without legal or other intervention from an outside source, you will not get one! The only steps you should attempt toward closure are legal ones.

    Report the crime — if their behavior is actually a crime in your state. If it's not, get busy making it one! Contact the internet source where you found them. Document their actions and bring a civil suit if your state's statutes permit. (But be aware of the high costs and low likelihood of reimbursement for your losses.)

Unless you have children or business with the person who harmed you, walk away and block all contact. Exposure to them could draw you back into their web of deceit and make your recovery exponentially more difficult.

There is rarely an opportunity for meaningful closure with a catfish. If you have contact with them, they'll frequently "ghost" you: disappear and cut off all communication. Or they'll "gaslight" you: make you question your own sanity. They'll discredit you to your friends, family, co-workers, employer, and even the police. You know a terrible thing about their character, and they need to silence you so the rest of the world doesn't figure them out.

- **Get treatment**

    Look for a therapist who understands the intoxicating nature of sociopaths and has experience with C-PTSD, including current treatments such as EMDR and tapping. The therapist you choose must understand that you've been defrauded of sex, money, or other assets, misused as a short-cut for immigration status, or harmed in a myriad of other ways. Find a therapist who validates, not dismisses, your emotions.

    As the therapeutic community becomes more aware, you should be able to locate a practitioner who's been trained to help clients recover from what Dr. Christine Louis De Canonville refers to as NVS.

    Sexually exploited victims need to find their way back to

reality and self-esteem. If this is you and you're unable to afford private help, seek care through support groups and the low cost/no cost mental health clinics at major hospitals.

- ***Disengage from folks who blame you.***

    No one *consents* to a deed when their permission is tricked from them through treachery. The blame for fraud rests on the shoulders of the offender, not the victim. Anyone can be fooled when the wrongdoer is an accomplished liar.

    Don't keep people in your support group who try to shame you. You learned the hard lesson that not everyone can be trusted. Don't confuse your need to be more circumspect in the future with blame for having been ripped off in the past. And don't tolerate anyone else doing so, either.

    Block the heartless words "Just get over it," "Move on," and "Don't *let* this affect you," from your mind. You are not "letting" it affect you. It simply *is* affecting you — not because you're weak, but because you're human.

    You need to surround yourself with people who possess the patience and love to support your healing. Your road toward recovery can be a long and difficult one. And it's one you'll need to travel down on your own, personal timetable.

- ***Become your best friend***

    1. Feed yourself healthy food.
    2. Force yourself to exercise in order to raise your endorphin levels. Doing so will help offset the loss of romantic chemistry that keeps you feeling attached.

3. Maintain a sleep routine with adequate, healing rest, but don't allow yourself to hide in your bedroom.

4. Do what makes you feel good about yourself! And don't feel you need to apologize for it.

5. Spend time with emotionally supportive family and friends. The enjoyment of fulfilling relationships is another antidote to the sudden withdrawal of romantic brain chemistry.

- ***Regaining trust in yourself is a step-by-step process***

    You need to crawl before you can run again. Now that you're wiser, you can put your knowledge to good use. Don't be afraid of being cautious. People often lament their loss of trust, but a reasonable level of fear will keep you safe in the future. Fear is wisdom in the face of danger.

    You can begin to restore faith in yourself by making commitments to yourself and living up to them. Start by making a list of what you need to accomplish that very day. Check off each task as you complete it. At the end of the day, review how much you were able to achieve. Begin each morning by going through the same process. Both by having stayed true to your commitments and by achieving the tasks you set out to do, you'll begin to restore your faith in yourself.

    Once you can get through a daily list of tasks, set longer-term goals. Write them down and work each day toward reaching them. Set a completion date and live up to it. Don't be disheartened by your misses. Everyone can succeed if we don't let our failures stop us. Get back on the path and try again.

- *Understand rumination — what it is, why it happens, and how to stop it*

    Because people with emotional empathy have difficulty imagining that people without empathy actually exist, they'll spend countless hours thinking about their loss and rehashing what they could have or should have done differently to salvage the relationship. "If only I would have done —" or, "If only he understood that —" are thoughts that plague them for hours on end. It's hard for victims to grasp that what was so real and intense for them was simply a cat-and-mouse game for the offender. The tug of chemical addiction to a romance partner keeps the victim rooted in feelings of love, even while feeling defiled.

    If it happens to you, you'll play the broken record of your relationship over and over in your mind. If you recognize you were just being used, you can detach, but the brain chemistry Mother Nature endowed you with works hard to keep you from dealing with the truth and walking away.

    You'll need to exercise tremendous willpower over your brain chemistry to stop yourself from this non-productive, repetitive thought process. One way to do this is to write down the relationship's history. Doing so frees you from having to keep the thoughts ever-present in your mind. Once written, you can safely tuck your thoughts away knowing you can take them out, at will, anytime you want. Writing everything down also helps you make greater sense of what happened.

    Each day, you'll need to make a concerted effort to put a

time limit on how long you'll allow yourself to dwell on the past. Shorten that timeframe every few days until you've whittled it down to an hour. Before you know it, you'll have trained your brain to dismiss the thoughts whenever you choose. And you won't want to give the person who harmed you a single second of space in your brain.

- *Learn about character disorder.*

    Reading and learning about sociopaths and what makes them tick is a must. It will help you come to terms with the scam you actually experienced. Educating yourself will enable you to live in reality and break free from the addiction you're experiencing. You'll find excellent research choices in the "Resources" section of this book.

- *Force yourself back into the world!*

    Do things you love. Remind yourself of the value in your life. Plan moments of enjoyment with friends, with family, or alone, taking in music, art, sports, or whatever makes you happy. Remind yourself that your episode with a scammer is not who you are; it's what happened to you. It does not have to define you.

- *Volunteer*

    There is nothing faster or better at rebuilding self-esteem than helping someone else. Doing so will empower you! It can also put you in the company of like-minded people who care about others — a place where you can feel safe once again.

    Become an advocate for people who have been scammed as

you were. Use your newly found knowledge to champion laws against catfish profiling and romance scams in your state or jurisdiction, and lend comfort to others who've been harmed.

Maybe you're not the victim; maybe you're watching a loved one go through the torment of scam withdrawal. Understand that they're not rehashing their pain over and over again because they choose to. They're doing so because they're experiencing an emotional/chemical addiction, and they're stuck in rumination. They need help, patience, and emotional support.

An old but appropriate axiom expresses what a "sexploitation" victim needs from the people around them:

"When you cry, your friends will try to cheer you up, but people who love you will give you a shoulder to cry on."

Victims need both friends and loved ones around them. Each has an important role in their recovery.

When Lies Become Fraud

Fraud is the most frequently committed crime in the US. It is by far the largest section of all crimes listed in penal codes throughout the country. In insurance fraud alone, over $80 billion in assets are lost each year. As previously discussed, in fraud cases, even though the victim provides agreement "on the face of it" their decision was induced by clouding their knowledge; therefore, their consent is considered "ineffective" under the law. According to Model Penal Code (MPC), which was written to standardize criminal law throughout the US, deception invalidates consent. All sexual activity requires valid consent.

Simply put, a catfish who engages a victim in sex, is conducting a covert form of sexual assault. Although the victim is unaware that they're being

defrauded at the time they provide cooperation, their permission is not legally viable as consent.

When a catfish deprives a victim of money or other assets, they are committing theft by fraud. When they sexually exploit the victim through the same means, they are committing sexual assault by fraud. If they induce a person to marry them to secure immigration status, they are committing immigration fraud. The US authorities; however, will only intercede in cases of asset fraud — and only rarely. Most states don't presently have statutes to prosecute sexual assault by fraud or the sexual defilement of marriage/immigration fraud.

Other countries are far more diligent in protecting victims. Sexual assault by fraud is a criminal and punishable offense in many parts of the world. Three such cases are pending in India at the time of this writing.

In November 2015, Nabam Rebia, the Speaker of the Assembly in the northeastern state of Arunachal Pradesh, was charged with physical and mental assault based on his "false promise to marry" his live-in girlfriend of four years. The police issued a First Information Report (FIR), which enables them to arrest without a warrant, based on the victim's complaints. FIRs can only be filed when the authorities believe that a *cognizable* crime has been committed.

The complainant cited false promises to marry her since 2011 and several instances of emotional harm, including damaging her reputation and making her the victim of scorn. The specific charges were cheating, breach of trust, and fraud. Members of Rebia's family were also charged for engaging in a disinformation campaign.

On September 25, 2015, in Canberra, Australia, Billy Tamiwawy was convicted of *sexual intercourse without consent*. Passing himself off as a woman named Tayla Edwards on Facebook, he tricked a teenage boy into having sex with him. Tamiwawy was sentenced to four years and ten months in prison.

On October 30, 2015, a Chinese court in Zhuhai, in southern Guangdong Province, convicted Wu Zeheng of multiple crimes. He was the leader of Hua Zang Dharma, a Buddhist-inspired cult. Among his offenses was rape by perpetrating a hoax. He had misused his holy status to trick women into believing that engaging in sex with him would imbue them with supernatural powers.

The Impact of MPC

Each state creates its own penal code; therefore crimes and their punishments differ from state to state. But MPC serves as a guide that lawmakers can rely on. Its Global Consent provision states, **"Consent is ineffective if induced by force, duress, or deception."**

In 2014, in Burlington County, New Jersey, when notorious catfish, William Allen Jordan, was caught, Assistant District Attorney Steve Eife failed to use the appropriate NJ statute to prosecute him for sexual assault. Jordan had embroiled the victim in an elaborate romance scam based on a totally false internet dating profile. Instead of simply charging sexual assault based on Jordan's deception, Eife insisted on charging "sexual assault by coercion," which could not possibly secure an indictment from the grand jury. Jordan had not used coercion which, in New Jersey's penal code, requires the threat of harm.

I had advocated for the victim in order to get the police to act. She'd read my book, *Carnal Abuse by Deceit,* which explained sexual assault by fraud and identified the act as "CAD" behavior. Two days after our visit to her precinct, Jordan was arrested.

When Eife insisted on pursuing the "sexual assault by coercion" charge, I attempted to change his mind. He moved the case forward without making the needed adjustment and, indeed, the grand jury failed to indict. Along the way, I learned that the prosecutor's office was aware that the victim intended to write a book about her case and they were loath to get involved at all. In fact, the judge at her hearing for a restraining order, tore her heart out stating he'd have to lock up half the college students in the country if Jordan's actions were considered a crime. I got the distinct impression that Eife's decision not to use a more appropriate charge was motivated by a desire to shoot this case in its foot.

On the day Jordan was sentenced for other crimes against the victim, I had a brief conversation with Eife and asked him why he'd insisted on using "coercion" rather than the Model Penal Code definition of "consent." He argued that the consent definition was not the same in New Jersey law, so I went back and checked my research. Here's what the New Jersey Penal Code actually says about consent. You be the judge!

<u>Consent is ineffective,</u> *unless otherwise provided, if it is given by a person who is induced by force, duress, or* **<u>deception</u>***, or by a person who is legally incompetent or otherwise unable to judge the harmfulness of the conduct. N.J.S.A. 2C:2-10c.*

As I'd hoped when I initially got involved in the case, the media attention attracted the interest of a legislator. Assemblyman Troy Singleton reached out to the victim, who lived in his district. He submitted NJ Assembly Bill #3908, Sexual Assault by Fraud. It was a noble effort on his part but received considerable negative backlash in the media. The language the victim had insisted on was far too broad. She had copied it from Tennessee's law, against my advice. Also against my advice and the advice of others who had previously influenced legislative changes in New Jersey, no press conference was held and no press kit was issued. Bill #3908 died in committee without even reaching the floor of the Assembly for a hearing.

Singleton dropped his bill into the hopper on the Assembly's floor on November 14, 2014. It was just a few days short of a year from when *Carnal Abuse by Deceit* was released. Before the ink on the bill was dry, I began receiving phone calls from the media. Because there had been no press conference, the negatives the press and public invented quickly spun out of control. A wave of damning backlash hit my blog from all around the world. I was accused of being a "feminazi" and a host of other colorful names. But by listening to the objections and studying the concerns of "nay-sayers," I fashioned language that I believe can address the need, and I've submitted my recommendations to Asm. Singleton and other legislators in NJ and additional states.

In order to enact a law to prevent romance fraud, society needs to understand the concept of *assent vs. consent* and the responsibility of victims to behave as a *reasonable person* would do, consistent with the behavior required in all crimes *against the person*. The law would convey the need for significant proof in order to bring about an arrest and prevent people from filing arbitrary claims, and revenge claims, that would be considered *de minimus* (frivolous). In all criminal trials; however, decisions of law are made by the judge while decisions pertaining to the facts of the case are made by the jury.

The definition of fraud

Fraud is not simply a crime that stands alone. It is a tool that is used as a covert (underhanded) weapon of choice by many criminals. Crimes involving fraud punish offenders according to the harm or loss the victim endures such as "theft by fraud." Only three states in the US, Tennessee, Alabama and Missouri have comprehensive laws to punish "sexual assault by fraud."

The two basic types of fraud addressed in "sexual assault by fraud" laws are *fraud in the factum,* which means lying about the action itself, or *fraud in the inducement,* lying about the intent or identity of the actor. For example, on April 27 2016, Dr. Ho Yin (Aaron) Shiu went on trial in Worcester, Massachusetts. Dr. Shiu is alleged to have inserted his finger into the genitals of his female patient on the premise that he was conducting a medically necessary examination. The woman's medical complaint was a spinal injury. He is also charged with inappropriately fondling her breasts by the same ruse. More than one victim came forward to file charges against Shiu. His case is a prime example of *fraud in the factum*. He can no longer practice medicine in the state of Massachusetts. He moved to New Jersey where he is eligible to practice.

Ironically, just down the road in Middlesex County, in July, 2016, District Attorney Marian Ryan declined to arrest Dr. Roger Hardy who was accused of committing unlawful sexual touching. Hardy had a long history of allegations of similar behavior that had never been prosecuted. DA Ryan claimed that "consent" had been achieved even though the victim thought the doctor was going to medically examine her, not sexually manipulate her genitals. Her decision to decline prosecution clearly shows her belief that MA judges would interpret the victim's "assent" as "consent."

Another case of *fraud in the factum* was filed on April 11, 2016, in Morgan Hill, California. Gym owner and trainer, David Wolfsmith, was arrested for "sexual battery by fraud" for deceiving his victims about the nature of his actions.

Lies of identity or intent are *fraud in the inducement*. Lies of intent are extremely difficult to prove because the offender could easily say, "I changed my mind." If a person who is already married promises marriage to someone else; however, their dishonesty is obvious.

Lies of identity, *false pretense* or *false personation*, can unequivocally be proven by the profile the offender wrote and posted on an e-dating site in order to sexploit the victim. When a person meets someone through internet dating or receives identity information via any type of technology, they should save the data.

The following is the definition of *fraud* that law school students learn very early-on in their studies:

1. The offender lies.
2. They know they're lying.

3. They expect their victim to rely on their lie.
4. The victim, in fact, relies on their lie.
5. The victim suffers harm resulting from 1-4.

A lie is a lie, and possibly, a crime

People are defrauded of sex each and every day. For many, their lives are shattered because a self-indulgent person thought of sex as an entitlement, not as a privilege. Because this crime involves the victim's reproductive organs, pregnancy can result. When that's the case, the victim will be reminded of the heinous depravation of the offender for the rest of their life, and can also suffer harmful financial consequences. The impacts on the child can be immense.

Every human being has the unequivocal right to exercise self-determination over their reproductive organs, and no one has the right to sexually exploit them, regardless of how easily they can do so. When it comes to sex, every human being should be able to select what *actions* and *actors* they allow.

In a murder case, the size of the offender's gun is irrelevant. And the size of the offender's lie, when snagging a victim, is not relevant either. It's the impact of the gun, and the impact of the lie on the victim, that makes using either type of weapon a crime. Because of their believability factor, smaller lies can be especially devious and deceptive.

In my case, the predator who sexually assaulted me over the course of three years lied about his age, his religion, his military background, his education, and his marital status. There was nothing flamboyant, strange, or unbelievable about anything he said.

He made himself older, not younger. It was easy to do because he was prematurely grey. He said he had a degree in accounting from New York University. In truth, he was a high school dropout.

Anyone who knows me for more than 32 seconds would tell you that I'm neither a stupid nor gullible woman. I wasn't needy. I was an independent career woman; my employer trusted me to make multi-million dollar decisions each day.

I was deeply in love with him, but the man I loved didn't really exist. I became pregnant with his child before learning about any of his lies. And I was not the only woman he impregnated by scamming her. Most sexual predators target multiple victims with absolutely no remorse.

Violence is an aggravated form of rape that deserves a far greater consequence than any other type of sexual assault. But all sexual assaults, including those that use lies to manipulate decisions, are human rights violations and should be punishable when the victim has a reasonable basis for believing the lies, and there is sufficient proof to convict the offender.

Enacting a Romance Scam Law

Not every case of sexual assault will meet the required criteria to prosecute. In Tennessee which has the broadest ability to litigate, only two convictions have resulted: State vs. Mitchell, 1999, and State vs. Brigman, 2003. The bar to secure a conviction in any sexual assault by fraud case is, indeed, very high. Enacting legislation; however, will enable society to understand the hideousness of the behavior, deter sexual predators, and diminish the extraordinary volume of this crime.

The *It's On Us Pledge* to curb college campus rape, supported by US President Barack Obama and Vice President Joseph Biden, states: *"Non-consensual sex is sexual assault."*

This clause clearly shows that agreement, in sexual relations, is set at the higher level of consent, not the lower level of assent.

Back in 1947, the Nuremberg trials took place to address inhumane medical experiments that were performed on 3,500,000 prisoners in German concentration camps during World War II. The federal Nuremberg Code was established to create an ethical standard by which experiments with human subjects can take place. As a result of this code, an entire series of regulations was created to identify and ensure human rights during medical experiments. The US Government's *Code of Regulations* states those rules in 45 CFR 46.116 - General Requirements For Informed Consent. Colleges and universities conducting such experiments write specific requirements using the basic principles of Nuremberg Code.

On August 27, 2015, *The Institutional Review Board* for the University of Alaska, Fairbanks, published its policy that distinguishes between assent and consent. It states: *"Work with children or adults not capable of giving consent requires the <u>consent</u> of the parent or legal guardian and the <u>assent</u> of the subject."*[12]

The University of Florida (UFL) also provides a similar explanation and a series of procedures for securing both consent and assent. Here is the language that UFL uses to describe what consent actually means to the US government, expressed in layman's terms:

> *"<u>The Nuremberg Code</u> states in pertinent part:*
>
> *The voluntary consent of the human subject is absolutely essential. This means that the person involved should have legal capacity to give consent; should be so situated as to be*

> able to exercise free power of choice without the intervention of any element of force, fraud, deceit, duress, overreaching, or other ulterior form of constraint or coercion; and should have sufficient knowledge and comprehension of the elements of the subject matter involved as to enable him to make an understanding and enlightened decision."

Neither morality nor the laws we use to codify criminal behavior should change from one situation to the next. What serves to describe consent in one circumstance is consistent in all circumstances. A lie is a lie, and consent is consent no matter in what context they are used.

The opposition to punishing this crime takes many forms, but largely, resistance results from a lack of awareness and understanding.

- *Opposition: "You can't arrest someone just because the victim changed their mind after the fact."*

    We don't consider being scammed "changing your mind," when you discover that a hoax deprived you of your assets, but when the scam is about sex, people seem to think that upon recognition, the victim simply **changed their mind**. Nothing could be further from the truth.

    By its very nature, the lie or "false pretense" by the offender negates the victim's choice. A victim who is embroiled in a sexual act without their consent, whether penetrated or penetrating, is sexually exploited. This means both men and women can be harmed this way. Neither will discover they were harmed until "after the fact," because the deed that harmed them took place prior to their discovery.

- *Opposition: "Sexual assault requires force or violence."*

  Every state's penal code recognizes that violence is not the only form of sexual assault or rape that exists. Statutory rape — conducting sexual intercourse with a minor, with or without the victim's permission (assent) — is unlawful. The person has not yet reached the age of reason. Even when they give permission, they can only provide assent, not consent; therefore, they are being violated. The same is true of sexual intercourse with a person who is too mentally incapacitated to provide consent.

  Statutory rape is a crime because the child is too young to "reason." Sexual assault by fraud is a crime because the offender deliberately undermined the victim's ability to reason, and they did so intentionally.

  Another form of sexual assault in which no violence need be present for prosecution is what society readily recognizes as *date rape.* When drugs or alcohol are involved, the person's consent is clouded in much the same way that false personation clouds the consent of a victim in sexual assault by fraud. The drug of choice; however, is lies that manipulate a person's response rather than drugs that are inhaled or ingested. Anything that scrambles a person's perception of either the act or the person performing the act makes intercourse a sexual assault, not seduction.

- *Opposition: "Wouldn't half the world go to jail if sexual assault by fraud laws were enacted?"*

    a. No. People would understand that the behavior is deplorable. Moral folks who hadn't previously understood would change their mindset. Today, we see slavery as an abomination, yet the US was once torn between supporters and abolitionists. Opinions change with enlightenment. Enacting new laws makes that happen.

Slavery, which was once commonplace, is now outlawed. All people can drink from all public water fountains and no one is relegated to the back of the bus. Laws change how society conducts itself.

b. Prosecuting all crimes requires proof. Simple *he-said, she-said* utterances, although they may very well be acts of sexual assault, are not always prosecutable. In fact, sexual assault by fraud is a very difficult case to prove. Unless the police, the prosecutor, and the grand jury all believe the case has sufficient merit, as in all crimes, no indictment will occur.

In catfish profiling, the offender has written specific false information with which they have deliberately set out to defraud their target. Their lies are documented and memorialized, and they have used a government-supported communication system to send their message to their victim. When their ruse is used to sexually engage the person, they are committing a covert and provable form of sexual assault.

Additionally, in order to prosecute a catfish, the victim would have to be judged as having behaved in a *reasonable* manner, a standard consistent with prosecution for all fraud crimes. If the victim is deemed reckless by the police or prosecutor, no charges would be filed.

- ***Opposition: "It's just lying. That's not fraud."***

Lying is not a crime. However, lies that create harm are fraud. When a catfish lies to violate the victim's right to self-determination over their reproductive organs, a crime is taking place.

- ***Opposition: "If you punish people for lying, you'll have to punish them for wearing makeup and other misleading appearance enhancements, like Spanx or high heels."***

The use of makeup as we know it dates back 6,000 years. Unless they have personal or religious reasons for not wearing makeup, the vast majority of modern women don't walk out the door in the morning without "their face on." Wearing makeup, in today's society, is a reasonable expectation.

If what a person looks like without makeup is important to a sexual partner, there's an easy remedy: ask them to remove it. Spanx and heels can come off as well, and often do.

On the other hand, when people tell lies to embroil you in sex, no matter how often or how plaintively you ask for the truth, they'll deceive you. Catfish laws are designed to provide justice when, despite reasonable due diligence, you were not able to discover the truth because the offender deliberately misled you.

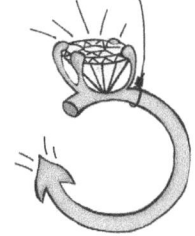

A woman I'll call Sunny filed a civil claim in Florida for both sexual assault by fraud and emotional distress. She'd met a man who claimed to be single. He led her to believe he intended to marry her. In fact, at the time, his wife of many years was pregnant with their third child.

The offender attempted to get Sunny's claims dismissed. Although the judge set aside the sexual assault by fraud charge because no such law exists in Florida, she allowed the claim of emotional distress to stand. She did so because the victim had been extremely direct with the offender; she'd conducted significant due-diligence when she met the man through an internet meet-up. As they got to know each other she confided that she'd had a difficult life and would be seriously harmed if he misrepresented himself to her. He lied despite her specific request for him not to do so.

Simply put...

Here are the basic reasons why sexual assault by false pretense or false personation is a crime:

- <u>Consent, not assent, must be given in every act of sex.</u> Deliberately tricking a person into thinking they're consenting to sex violates their reproductive organs and sexually exploits that victim.
- <u>All sex acts must include consent, not assent, to both the action and the actor.</u> Deceiving the victim about the action is fraud in the factum. Deceiving them about the person they engage in sex with is fraud in the inducement. No one has the right to induce sex through any form of trickery.

It's imperative that a person using false pretense in their dating profile straighten out their lies *before* engaging in sex. People use fraud to induce sex because they feel manipulation is their right. When they manipulate you for your money, they're risking jail time. When they manipulate you to sexually exploit you, they feel it's perfectly okay. It's not.

When catfish profiling laws exist in your location, whether or not a catfish goes to jail will depend on whether or not you can prove that they used false personation or false pretense to mislead you, and whether you behaved "reasonably" as required by your state or jurisdiction.

Until specific laws are passed to prosecute romance scams, seeking justice is extremely rare and difficult. In Alabama, defrauding someone of sex is a Class B misdemeanor called sexual misconduct; in Tennessee, defrauding someone of sexual intercourse is rape and sexual "touching" is sexual battery. Both are felonies.

In Missouri, using deception to induce sex is 2nd degree rape. Missouri's definition of "consent" indicates that "assent" does not constitute "consent" if induced by deception. The laws of Missouri could be used as a model for other states as they clearly indicate the role of "assent" and do not limit the term, "deception."

On October 21, 2015, I addressed a joint hearing conducted by the Consumer Frauds and Senior Frauds Commissions of New York State's Assembly in order to focus attention on this issue. The following is a portion of the statement I submitted during the hearing:

Assemblyman Members, Dinowitz, Cymbrowitz and Seawright:

Thank you for the opportunity to address you this morning.

Catfish are covert, rather than overt criminals. Instead of using a two-by-four to violently overcome a person's resistance, they use lies, charm, and romance as tools to defraud their victims.

Modern scientists are seriously examining the role brain chemistry such as oxytocin, vasopressin, serotonin, dopamine, and other neuropeptides and hormones play in making people trusting and loving human beings. Highly skilled scammers misuse a target's brain chemistry to attract and deceive them. They are masters at the laws of attraction. Tricking a person into sex stirs up their brain chemistry and makes them even more susceptible to financial or other losses.

Loneliness, naiveté, and gullibility are not crimes. Defrauding a person of assets or sex, or misusing them for marriage/immigration fraud is, and should be.

In all crimes of fraud, the offender knows they are defrauding, while their victim does not. The fact that the victim's recognition of the crime is delayed does not negate that a crime indeed took place. For example, it took Bernie Madoff's victims several years to recognize they'd been scammed.

I respectfully request that the State of New York

adopt the following measures to ensure the safety of all e-dating consumers, the old, the young, and everyone in between:

1. That dating sites operating in New York be required to display a warning saying "This site does not guarantee the credibility of any member's profile," and establish a hotline to report catfish profiles. They should be required to respond to the complainant's request within 24 hours.
2. That dating sites provide the following warning: "Before you engage in a financial exchange, intimacy, or aid in the immigration of anyone you meet on this site, conduct appropriate due diligence to determine that their facts are accurate, and exchange photo ID."
3. Make the distinction between violent rape and other types of sexual assaults (covert rapes) in New York State's penal codes. Change the wording in statutes that are not dealing with violent rape to "sexual assault." Violent rape is an aggravated form of sexual assault, but our penal code now recognizes several forms of covert rape in which no violence takes place. Undermining a person's consent in any way is a form of sexual assault on that victim, whether or not violence is the tool the offender uses.

Making the distinction between violent sexual assault and non-violent but covert sexual assault will make the concept clearer for the public.

4. Identify catfish profiling as "some factor" in statute 130.25 which reads "a person is guilty of rape [sexual assault] in the third degree when: he or she engages in sexual contact with another person without such person's consent where such lack of consent is by reason of false personation or false pretense or something other than incapacity to consent." In other words, the reason the victim does not consent could be because they are incapacitated, but also because they are tricked into consent. Rape in the third degree is a class E felony.

Ready, Set...Legal Action!

The following text for a "Sex Scam Law," is appropriate for the penal code of every state. Only minimal revisions are needed to adapt to code requirements that can differ from state to state. Using consistent wording can strengthen society's understanding.

I've modified the text for this recommendation from a catfish bill that was originally introduced in New York State in 2013 by Senator Greg Ball. Senator Ball subsequently retired from politics. The bill was brought to my attention by Kelley Cahill, the founder of ICheckMates, a much-needed and soon-to-be-launched service that will authenticate the identities of internet users.

SEX SCAM LAW

The People of the State of _____, represented in Senate and Assembly, do enact as follows:

SECTION 1

This act shall be known and may be cited as:

The Sexual Assault by False Personation or False Pretense Protection Act of 2017

1-1. In the state of _____, assent to sexual conduct does not qualify as consent when assent is induced by deception.

1-2. **Sexual Assault by False Personation or False Pretense,**
When the offender undermines the victim's right to knowledgeable consent regarding his or her reproductive organs, by using false statements, false documents, false electronic presentations, or elaborate hoaxes, and the victim has a reasonable basis to believe such false information, the offender has committed a Class E Felony punishable by 0 to 4 years of incarceration.

1-3. **Aggravated Sexual Assault by False Personation or False Pretense**
When the offender commits Sexual Assault by False Personation or False Pretense in connection

with another crime, such as defrauding the victim of assets or embroiling them in marriage fraud to secure immigration status, or when they have knowingly deceived the victim about their sexually transmittable disease, they have committed Aggravated Sexual Assault by False Personation or False Pretense, a Class C Felony punishable by 1 to 8 years of incarceration.

SECTION 2: DEFINITIONS

2-1. **Assent:** Superficial agreement which is given "on the face of it." Assent provides acquiescence and compliance, but lacks the characteristics of being <u>informed</u> and <u>knowledgeable</u> about the agreed upon action or actor.

2-2. **Consent:** Fully informed agreement which entails accurate knowledge of the action (fraud in the factum) and the actor (fraud in the inducement).

A person providing consent must have legal capacity to give consent; should be so situated as to be able to exercise free power of choice without the intervention of any element of force, fraud, deceit, duress, over-reaching, or other ulterior form of constraint or coercion; and should have sufficient knowledge and comprehension of the sexual partner and action taking place to enable her or him to make an understood and enlightened decision.

SECTION 3: JUSTIFICATION

3-1. The internet has spawned a new type of crime. Even e-dating operators admit that the number of dating site profiles containing lies constitutes over 50% of a site's content. There are no current protections in place to shield victims from this behavior, allowing romance scams to grow to epidemic proportions.

3-2. Studies have shown that the false impressions offenders create in order to seduce their victims can influence the victim's brain chemistry. And when those false impressions are not recognized by the victim prior to engaging in sex, the victim can only **assent** to the act; the victim cannot **consent** to the act.

3-3. The victim can suffer Complex Post Traumatic Stress Disorder (C-PTSD) and a sense of defilement, humiliation, and shame consistent with other types of sexual assault.

3-4. Punishing offenders for this offense will require significant proof of their intent to defraud and significant proof of a reasonable basis for belief on the part of the victim, thereby eliminating de minimus claims.

3-5. As a result of the deceit, victims of false personation or false pretense are left with emotional, mental, and financial scars. They often need therapy to recover.

3-6. Offenders who create fake profiles often target victims over long periods of time. The longer the hoax continues, the more deeply defiled and scarred the victim will feel.

3-7. Sex scams are a covert form of sexual assault. The offender uses the covert weapon of fraud instead of using an overt weapon such as violence.

3-8. Offenders target multiple victims either one-by-one, or concurrently, adding to the spread of sexually transmitted diseases.

3-9. Currently there is no specific law making this type of deceit a crime. This legislation establishes **Sexual Assault by False Personation and False Pretense** as a Class E Felony to hold accountable those who consciously deceive and lie to induce sex.

####

PENALTY FOR SEX SCAM CRIMES

As in all laws, punishment can vary according to the severity of the crime. Certainly, the punishment for non-violent sexual assault and violent sexual assault should not be the same. Class E Felonies are generally punished by 0-4 years of incarceration. The judge and jury can exercise discretion when handing down the offender's sentence. The minimum sentence; however, should include the following:

FIRST OFFENSE:

Sex offender list for 2 years, Fine of $25,000 and Community Service

- Society needs protection from the exploits of the offender. The victim has been sexually assaulted and their psyche will undergo considerable turmoil to recover their dignity and self-esteem. A reasonable amount of time in therapy will be two years. The offender should be cognizant of the harm they created for the same amount of time, and suffer a loss of face for the period. Therefore, they should be required to register as a sex offender for the two year <u>period</u>.
- **Therapy:** The cost of therapy for the victim should be borne by the offender for the two year period. A reasonable expense for that therapy would be $20,000.00; therefore, the offender should pay a fine in the amount of the therapy the victim needs.
- **Education:** Offenders must learn to identify and respect the law regarding "consent" in order to grasp how they should conduct themselves in the future. The state should create a teaching module and instruction. And the cost of that education should be borne by the offender in the amount of $5,000.
- For the two year period, the offender should be required to conduct strenuous community service.

SUBSEQUENT OR MULTIPLE OFFENSES, AND AGGRAVATED SEXUAL ASSAULT:

3 to 8 years of incarceration and Sex Offender Registry

- Repeat offenses should be treated as "aggravated."
- All cases in which the offender committed additional crimes against the victim such as grand theft, credit card fraud, theft by fraud or immigration fraud should be treated as "aggravated."

What Can You Do?

First off, reach out to your legislators and tell them how important enacting the catfish sex scam bill is to you. Locate a sponsor in your state's assembly and one in the senate. Campaign to get the law passed in your state. If you're a victim of a romance scam, be sure to tell them your story.

Truth in Romance Day

We have Valentine's Day for celebrating love. We have days to acknowledge Moms, Dads, and Grandparents. We even have days to recognize groundhogs. And did you know that September 24th is National Punctuation Day? It's  important to set a day aside to focus on the morality that's imperative in romantic and sexual relations, and give every couple the opportunity to exchange truthful information before untruths progress a minute longer.

June 15th is the day that all new romance and sexual partners should share ID and "'fess up" about any fiction they've told each other. If new romantic partners knew they had to "come clean" every June 15th, the rate of sex scams would drop. Offenders would understand from the get-go that they'd be found out.

People who've fallen prey to hoaxes know the horrid sense of defilement that accompanies what should be one of the most gratifying undertakings of our lives — finding an emotional and sexual partner. But all too many romance seekers become victimized by deceptions that undermine their sexual self-determination, exploit them, and crush their self-esteem in ways that can last a lifetime.

Separating someone with a pure heart from a scammer can often be addressed by checking their ID before the relationship proceeds to sexual intimacy. You should know, for a fact, who you're dealing with long before you're engaging in sex. For catfish who have snuck past your gates undetected, June 15th can be their day of reckoning.

Why is sharing ID so important?

Neither Tom Gatto (Steve Guida) nor Liam Allen (William Allen Jordan) used their real names to exploit their victims. Their targets would have known they were not who they claimed had they checked their IDs before engaging in sex. Knowing the accurate name of your romantic interest improves your chance of uncovering the truth.

Naysayers mock the idea of asking for ID; "You'll be locked in the heat of passion, reaching for zippers and unfastening hooks when you'll hear, 'Wait! I have to see your ID!' And you have to sign this document on the dotted line to attest to its authenticity!" Belittling new concepts is predictable behavior. Protecting yourself from a growing crime wave should become a common occurrence, especially in internet dating.

Scammers are loath to tell you their address, especially if they're married. And if they're 45, not 33 like they said, wouldn't you like to know? But you really shouldn't wait 'til your clothes are coming off to find out.

But it's so embarrassing and invasive to check ID, isn't it?

Sometimes the fear of looking "untrusting" holds people back from asking. And that's the kind of "emotional empathy" thought process that an offender is counting on. Think of it this way: wouldn't someone who cares about you and has been truthful with you want you to feel safe with them?

Valence effect refers to a normal tendency to think of positive rather than negative outcomes. Having a positive valence effect can inspire us to achieve greater heights than if we constantly focus on the negatives that are in front of us. Some would call positive valence "wishful thinking," but it sure comes in handy if we need to flee from a burning building or a capsizing boat! The optimism of the valence effect helps us think that a solution is around the corner when we're afraid. But con artists misuse our valence effect to fool us. Don't let your positive valence deter you from protecting yourself.

While you're looking at their driver's license, don't hesitate to ask for any other proofs you need, like the health test they told you they'd taken a couple of weeks ago. If they falsify or forge the documents they give you, and you rely on their false representation to engage in sex, they should be prosecuted.

What if they don't want to share their ID with you?

If the two of you have been intimate, and your belief is that you've embarked on an ongoing relationship, they should be eager to help you feel secure. If not, they're probably hiding something from you. You're better off knowing and walking away.

And the reward is?

Just as most special days call for unique gifts, like candy on Valentine's Day and flowers on Mother's Day, exchanging ID and *coming clean* on Truth in Romance Day is the perfect opportunity for a luxurious bubble bath for two, accompanied by a sprinkle of rose petals, some candles, and a chilled bottle of your favorite champagne. It's the perfect reward for respecting and building trust between you and your new romance partner.

When I was young and said something I shouldn't, my mother would reach for a horrible-tasting bar of soap. That and a swift trip through the exit door are appropriate consequences for those who fail their ID check.

Truth in Romance Day is designed to give you the support you need in order to satisfy your concerns and protect yourself. If you're newly in a relationship, and have yet to see the other person's ID, here's how you could introduce this concept......

You: I saw a great new idea for people who just got together like us! It's called "Truth in Romance Day." What do you think of people who lie to get laid?

Your mate: They're really heels! I'd never do that to you!

You: Great! I was hoping you'd feel that way! Is there anything that concerns you about what I've told you about myself? I'm happy to show you proof.

Your mate: Nope, I think you've been totally honest with me.

You: Excellent, 'cuz June 15th is the day when romantic partners around the world are going to share their IDs with each other, and I know that won't be a problem for us, right?

Up to this point, it's been pretty smooth sailing, right? But here are some of the many responses you can expect:

Your mate: That's a stupid idea. I'm amazed you'd expect me to do that!

Ooops...wrong answer! You've probably seen your first sign of deceit. You've offered a mutual sharing, not just an expectation of compliance. Resistance is probably a cover-up for a distortion their ID would uncover.

Your mate: I really don't think we're at a point where I want to share that information with you.

If you've had sex with this person, they're basically saying that it's "just sex" and there's no intimacy or relationship behind it. Better that you get the lay of the land today than proceed with false hopes! Do you really want to continue sharing your body and stimulating the brain chemistry of romantic attachment under this circumstance?

Your mate: It's that stupid feminist agenda. You're not a "feminazi," are you?

Morally bereft people use belittling to manipulate others. They engage in put-downs and name calling to throw you off track.

If the person's been honest with you and you have the basis of a loving foundation, there's no reason why they wouldn't want to share their ID with you, or show you proof regarding any other issues that concern you.

Your mate: You don't have "trust issues" do you?

In our technology driven society, fooling people from behind a veil of anonymity has become commonplace. It's necessary to protect yourself. It's just plain common sense!

Here's the answer that reflects a pure heart...

Your mate: I'm so happy we've found each other, and I'm honored you've chosen me to share with. I care about you and will do whatever it takes to build your trust.

You: Fabulous! The reward for sharing ID is a bubble bath for two and a bottle of champaign. I'm really looking forward to it! I'll bring the bubbles if you'll bring the bubbly!

Resources To Help You Unhook

Many supportive blogs deal with healing from toxic romances. Catfish offenders are frequently without empathy or conscience; therefore, internet sites focused on morality disorders provide concrete, useful information, including support and recovery guidance. Here are some outstanding choices:

Daily Strength: http://www.dailystrength.org/

- An online support community that deals with emotional and medical challenges with over 500 blog topics
- Contributors are medical professionals.
- This service provides advice, a hotline, and relief through journal writing.

Federal Bureau of Investigation Internet Crime Complaint Center (IC3): http://www.ic3.gov/default.aspx

- FBI's reporting site for internet crimes

LoveFraud: http://www.lovefraud.com

- Supportive healing blog for survivors of sociopathic abuse in romantic relationships
- Ongoing dialogue with other victims

Love. Life. Om. Mindfulness Coaching: http://lovelifeom.com/

- Mind and body healing for survivors of domestic violence, rape, and fraud
- Written from the perspective of a yoga specialist who fell prey to a romance scam

Let Me Reach: http://letmereach.com/

- Counseling to aid in recovery from narcissistic abuse
- Recovery and "No Contact" coaching

Marriage Immigration Fraud Worldwide Facebook Page: https://www.facebook.com/Marriage-Immigration-Fraud-Worldwide-557070931017670/

- Victims share their experiences when they've been duped into marriage/immigration scams.
- Focuses on legal remedies and healing

Narcissistic Behavior: http://www.NarcissisticBehavior.net

- Recovery advice for victims of narcissistic abuse
- Written by a professional psychologist who not only

conducts an individual therapy practice but also trains mental health professionals how to recognize and treat NVS

Psychiatric Times: http://www.psychiatrictimes.com/

- Updates on psychiatric treatments and findings
- Written by mental health professionals for mental health professionals

RAINN: https://rainn.org/

- The Rape Abuse and Incest National Network
- Provides an online hotline and an extensive, international database of real-world supports for rape survivors

ScamWatch:https://www.scamwatch.gov.au/ types-of-scams/dating-romance

- Up-to-date information on scams, including romance scams and resources for reporting incidents. Directed to residents in Australia and New Zealand, but their information applies worldwide.
- Overseen by the Australian Competition and Consumer Commission of the Autralasian Consumer Frauds Taskforce

Stop Rape By Fraud: http://www.StopRapeByFraud.com

- Discusses the laws on sexual assault and catfish profiling and advocates for the passage of legislation. It also clarifies the harmful effects of defilement and provides steps for healing and enlightenment.
- Focuses on the criminal elements in catfish profiling and

sexual assault by fraud. Also provides healing strategies and knowledge for victims and their support groups.

Tea Consent:

https://www.youtube.com/watch?v=oQbei5JGiT8

- The very best and most enlightening explanation of sexual "consent" ever!

By passing sex scam laws and expanding media focus, society's grasp of sexual assault by false pretense or false personation is destined to grow. You can play an important role in raising awareness and bringing about change.

If you're the victim of a romance scam, tell your story! Find your local legislators. Share this book with them! Insist they pass the law to protect the residents of your state because anyone who engages in romance can be scammed! Don't let it happen to you or someone you care about! Help get the law passed today!

Recommended Reading

Ready to heal? Several books have been written on the subject of sociopaths and recovery from victimization. Here are a few notable ones:

- *Betrayal Bond: Breaking Free of Exploitive Relationships,* Patrick Carnes, Ph.D.
- *Carnal Abuse by Deceit: How a Predator's Lies Became Rape,* Joyce M. Short
- *How to Do "No Contact" Like a Boss,* Kim Saeed
- *In Sheep's Clothing: Understanding and Dealing with Manipulative People,* George K. Simon Jr.
- *Red Flags of Love Fraud — 10 Signs You're Dating a Sociopath,* Donna Anderson
- *Soul Vampires: Reclaiming Your Lifeblood After Narcissistic Abuse,* Dr. Andrea Schneider
- *The Forgiveness Myth: How to Heal Your Hurts, Move On and Be Happy Again When You Can't — or Won't — Forgive,* Gary Egeberg and Wayne Raiter
- *The Moral Molecule,* Paul Zak, Ph.D.
- *The Sociopath Next Door,* Martha Stout, Ph.D.
- *The Three Faces of Evil: Unmasking the Full Spectrum of Narcissistic Abuse,* Dr. Christine Louis de Canonville
- *Unashamed Voices: True Stories Written by Survivors of Domestic Violence, Rape and Fraud: Exposing Sociopaths in Our Midst,* Paula Carasquillo, MA
- *Without Conscience: The Disturbing World of the Psychopaths Among Us,* Robert Hare, Ph.D.

Definitions

Anti-Social Personality Disorder (ASPD) – a dysfunctional and chronic mental disorder in which people are destructive, disregard the rights of others, and pay little attention to right and wrong. They are frequently pathological liars, impulsive, violent, and abuse drugs or alcohol. ASPD is one of several disorders that fall under the overall umbrella of *Cluster B* in the DSM.

Assent – Superficial agreement which is given "on the face of it." Assent provides acquiescence and compliance, but lacks the characteristics of being informed and knowledgeable about the agreed upon action.

At-risk for character disorder – A term used to describe children with a character disordered parent. While a child may not develop a character disorder, their DNA places them "at risk" for the possibility.

Borderline Personality Disorder (BPD) – A dysfunctional and chronic mental disorder in which people are oversensitive, over-reactive, and frequently cause rifts and splits with family members and loved ones. Treatments vary in approach from dealing with the instability of attachment (MBT) to ameliorating emotional dysregulation (DBT).

CAD- *v.* The act of carnal abuse by deceit, scamming for sex. *n.* The perpetrator of an act of carnal abuse by deceit, someone who scams for sex.

Catfish Profile – An online profile containing fictitious information intended to attract victims into a romance scam.

Cluster B Personality Disorder[13] – Contained in DSM, a mental dysfunction categorized by chronically dramatic, emotional and erratic interactions with others, with limited or no conscience. The divisions within Cluster B are Anti-Social Personality Disorder, Narcissistic Personality Disorder, Histrionic Personality Disorder and Borderline Personality Disorder. Impulse control and poor emotional regulation are common factors in each of the disorders. The general public generically uses the terms *psychopath* and *sociopath* to describe people who have these conditions.

Complex Post Traumatic Stress Disorder (C-PTSD) – A mental condition resulting from long-term exposure to derisive behavior such as emotional abuse, sexual abuse, domestic abuse, or coercive control, from which the victim sees no short-term possibility of escape. Symptoms can include self-destructive behaviors, hyper anxiety, and fear of being unworthy or incompetent.

Coercive Control – Actions using covert tactics to manipulate and deprive a person of their human rights; a form of domestic or emotional abuse.

Consent – Fully informed agreement which entails accurate knowledge of the action (fraud in the factum) and the actor (fraud in the inducement). A person providing consent must have legal capacity to give consent; should be so situated as to be able to exercise free power of choice without the intervention of any element of force, fraud, deceit, duress, over-reaching, or other ulterior form of constraint or coercion; and should have sufficient knowledge and comprehension of the sexual partner and action taking place to enable her or him to make an understood and enlightened decision.

Dark Triad – Three personality types that criminologists distinguish as malevolent. They include Narcissism, Machiavellianism (Malignant Narcissism), and Psychopathy.

Dialectical Behavioral Therapy (DBT) – A therapy approach for treating Borderline Personality Disorder that focuses on emotional dysregulation.

Disinformation campaign – The act of spreading false information in order to discredit or defame a person.

Domestic Violence – Various types of assault between two intimate partners, including intimidation, violence, sexual assault, emotional abuse, or other forms of torment to dominate and control.

DSM – *Diagnostic and Statistical Manual of Mental Disorders*, published by the American Psychiatric Association and used by mental health professionals throughout the US and in many other areas of the world.

EMDR – Eye Movement Desensitization and Reprocessing Therapy. An integrative psychotherapy protocol that relieves the stress of traumatic memories and manages PTSD, C-PTSD, and other trauma and anxiety-related symptoms.

Empathy – The sensitivity that exists in the human brain that guides our interactions with others and is the basis for conscience. There are three distinct forms:

- Cognitive – being aware of the emotions of others

- Emotional (Affective) – feeling a kinship with the emotions of others
- Compassionate – the ability to utilize information gained from cognitive and emotional empathy to benefit others

Gaslight – A discrediting technique used to undermine a person's self-esteem and produce doubt over their sanity.

Genetics – The passing along of certain traits through a person's genes.

Malignant Narcissism – Although this severe mental condition does not appear in the DSM, criminologists and mental health practitioners consider Malignant Narcissism to be a heightened level of NPD in which the person is not only grandiose but also paranoid and sadistic. Malignant Narcissism, also called Machiavellianism, is included in the Dark Triad.

Mentalization Based Treatment (MBT) – A treatment approach for Borderline Personality Disorder that focuses on the instability of attachment and mentalization as the core dysfunction.

Narcissistic Personality Disorder (NPD) – A dysfunctional and chronic mental disorder in which the person displays high levels of grandiosity and low levels of empathy. Someone with this condition may try to undermine others in order to self-aggrandize with no regard for the damage they cause. It is believed that people with NPD are masking an extreme level of insecurity. NPD falls under the umbrella of Cluster B Personality Disorder in the DSM.

Narcissistic Victim Syndrome (NVS) – The group of

symptoms that result from continued exposure to narcissistic abuse.

Neuropeptides – Small signaling molecules that stimulate brain activity.

Nigerian or 419 Scams[14] – Online romance scams that originate in Nigeria or Ghana. They are so prevalent that the US Embassy issued a warning to US citizens containing the following red flags:

- You met a friend/fiancé online
- You've never met face-to-face
- Your correspondent professed love at warp speed
- Your friend/fiancé is plagued with medical problems requiring loans from you
- You are promised repayment upon the inheritance of alluvial gold or gems
- You've sent large sums for visas or plane tickets but the person cannot seem to make it out of Ghana
- When your friend does try to leave the country, h/she is detained by immigration officials demanding payment or bribes
- Your correspondent consistently uses lower case "i's" and/or grammar not in keeping with their supposed life station or education level

Oxytocin – A neuropeptide stimulated by positive social interaction such as hugs, sex, or other physical closeness, created in the pituitary of mammals to promote trust, bonding, nursing between infants and their mothers, and additional benefits.

Pity-Play – Manipulative device used to elicit feelings of sympathy in order to induce a desired behavior.

Post Traumatic Stress Disorder (PTSD) – A mental state that results from exposure to a traumatic event or events. Generally associated with the horrors of warfare, PTSD can affect anyone who is the victim or observer of a terrifying act.

Psychopathy – A term used in the DSM to characterize morality disordered people within Cluster B who are particularly malevolent and plotting in their behavior. The characteristics of psychopaths and sociopaths are extremely similar in many ways. Both fail to heed the laws of society. They have no remorse or guilt over their misdeeds. They have no regard for the rights of other people and will use violence and manipulation to get what they want. Their morally bereft behavior is thought to be the result of innate brain dysfunction that is genetic in nature.

Rape – Once perceived solely as a sexual conquest resulting from the use of violence, rape is now viewed by enlightened society as the act of undermining a person's self-determination over their reproductive organs, by any means, in order to sexually exploit them. In addition to the physical violation of the victim's body, rape is an act that causes shame, humiliation, and extreme emotional distress to the victim.

Rape Trauma Syndrome (RTS) – a condition affecting rape victims in which the person feels humiliated and ashamed by having been sexually exploited. RTS is not a mental illness or disorder. It is a typical response to rape (or sexual assault). RTS caused by violent rape affects the victim physically, psychologically and behaviorally. RTS caused by non-violent forms of rape affects the victim psychologically and behaviorally.

Romance Scam – A hoax or ruse aimed at defrauding the victim of emotions and/or sex. Romance scams are frequently used as a covert weapon to blind the victim to additional underhanded actions.

Rumination – Repetitious thoughts caused by preoccupation with past events; these thoughts are difficult for the sufferer to control or prevent. Rumination often results from the cessation of emotional attachments when no closure takes place.

Scam – A hoax or ruse aimed at defrauding the victim.

Sexploitation – Sexually exploiting a person by any means.

Sexual Assault – The act of engaging in sexual activity by undermining a person's self-determination over their reproductive organs. Sexual assault is the sexual exploitation of another and causes shame and humiliation to the victim.

Sexual Battery – a term used in the penal codes of several states when referring to sexual assaults.

Sexual Exploitation – Touching the reproductive organs of another person without their consent which renders shame and humiliation.

Sexual Misconduct – Behavior of a sexual nature in which the offender has deprived the victim of knowing consent regarding their actions.

Snag – Sexual exploitation and misconduct taking place when a predator appears to be seducing but, in fact, is sexually assaulting by the use of false pretense or deception.

Sociopathy – A term used in the DSM to characterize morality disordered people within Cluster B who are malicious and impulsive in their behavior. The characteristics of sociopaths and psychopaths are similar in many ways: they both fail to heed the laws of society. They have no remorse or guilt over their misdeeds. They have no regard for the rights of others and will use violence and manipulation to get what they want. Sociopathy is thought to evolve due to exposure to abusive treatment during early development.

Tapping Therapy (also known as Emotional Freedom Techniques (EFT) and Meridian Tapping Techniques (MTT)) – A technique designed to work like emotional acupuncture to bridge the divide between insights gained in psychotherapy and their application in real life.

Notes

1. http://www.huffingtonpost.com/greg-hodge/online-dating-lies_b_1930053.html
2. Stephenson, Debbie. "Spear Phishing: Who's Getting Caught?". Firmex. Retrieved July 27, 2014.
3. The Urban Dictionary http://www.urbandictionary.com/define.php?term=catfish
4. https://www.scamwatch.gov.au/types-of-scams/dating-romance
5. https://www.fbi.gov/audio-repository/news-podcasts-thisweek-romance-scams.mp3/view
6. *Journal of Traumatic Stress*, Volume 5, 1992, Judith Lewis Herman, *Complex PTSD: A Syndrome in Survivors of Prolonged and Repeated Trauma* http://www.readcube.com/articles/10.1002%2Fjts.2490050305?r3_referer=wol&tracking_action=preview_click&show_checkout=1&purchase_referrer=onlinelibrary.wiley.com&purchase_site_license=LICENSE_DENIED_NO_CUSTOMER
7. *Boxed In,* New York Civil Liberties Union, August, 2012 http://www.nyclu.org/files/publications/nyclu_boxedin_FINAL.pdf
8. *The London Daily Telegraph,* Sarah Knapton, Science Editor http://www.telegraph.co.uk/news/science/science-news/11542075/Why-humans-love-pet-dogs-as-much-as-their-children.html

9. *Science/AAAS* http://www.sciencemag.org/search?author1=Miho+Nagasawa&sortspec=date&submit=Submit
10. Revenge Porn Takes Center Stage http://rapebyfraud.com/2016/01/26/revenge-porn-takes-center-stage-you-can-help/
11. Inside Science TV, *Love Highs and Lows,* Ali Jennings, February 10, 2016 https://www.insidescience.org/content/love-highs-and-lows/3641
12. University of Alaska Fairbanks, *Institutional Review Board,* August 27, 2015 http://www.uaf.edu/irb/faqs/consent-and-assent/
13. https://www.mentalhelp.net/articles/dsm-5-the-ten-personality-disorders-cluster-b/
14. http://ghana.usembassy.gov/romance_scam.html

www.ingramcontent.com/pod-product-compliance
Lightning Source LLC
Chambersburg PA
CBHW071309060426
42444CB00034B/1746